HOW TO
BRING UP BABY

SAM MARTIN

Sam Martin is a dad. His other accomplishments include being the bestselling author of *How to Mow the Lawn* and *How to Keep House*. When his first child was born he was working as a senior editor at *This Old House* magazine in New York. He lives in Texas with his wife, Denise, and sons, Ford and Wren.

HOW TO
BRING UP BABY

SAM MARTIN

KEY PORTER BOOKS

This edition published by Key Porter Books by arrangement with Elwin Street Limited

2006 Key Porter Books

Copyright © 2006 by Elwin Street Limited

Conceived and produced by
Elwin Street Limited
79 St John Street
London EC1M 4NR
www.elwinstreet.com

Library and Archives Canada Cataloguing in Publication

Martin, Sam
    How to bring up baby / Sam Martin.

Includes index.
ISBN 1-55263-764-6

    1. Infants—Care. 2. Father and Infant. I. Title.

HQ756.M35 2006   649'.122

C2005-903905-1

ONTARIO ARTS COUNCIL
CONSEIL DES ARTS DE L'ONTARIO

THE CANADA COUNCIL | LE CONSEIL DES ARTS
FOR THE ARTS | DU CANADA
SINCE 1957 | DEPUIS 1957

The publisher gratefully acknowledges the support of the Canada Council for the Arts and the Ontario Arts Council for its publishing program. We acknowledge the support of the Government of Ontario through the Ontario Media Development Corporation's Ontario Book Initiative.

We acknowledge the financial support of the Government of Canada through the Book Publishing Industry Development Program (BPIDP) for our publishing activities.

Key Porter Books Limited
Six Adelaide Street East, Tenth Floor
Toronto, Ontario
Canada M5C 1H6

www.keyporter.com

Designed by Jon Wainwright, Alchemedia Design
Illustration by David Eaton and Richard Burgess
Photographs courtesy Hulton Archive, Getty Images

Printed and bound in Singapore

05 06 07 08 09 5 4 3 2 1

Disclaimer: While every effort has been made to ensure that the content of this book is technically accurate and as sound as possible, neither the author nor the publishers can accept responsibility for any injury or loss sustained as a result of this material. As with all matters concerning health, and especially the health of infants, the instructions and advice in this book are in no way intended as a substitute for medical counseling.

CONTENTS

INTRODUCTION 6

CHAPTER 1:
YOU'RE HAVING A BABY! 13

CHAPTER 2:
LIFE WILL NEVER BE THE SAME 27

CHAPTER 3:
KEEPING BABY SAFE 41

CHAPTER 4:
SOME IMPORTANT BASICS 63

CHAPTER 5:
SNIFFS AND COUGHS (AND HOW TO DEAL WITH THEM) 85

CHAPTER 6:
THE CRYING GAME 107

CHAPTER 7:
PLAYTIME! (FOR YOU AND BABY) 115

CHAPTER 8:
TIME FOR MOM AND TIME FOR DAD 127

INDEX 142

INTRODUCTION

Okay guys, here we go. There are seven words that need to sink in here: You are going to be a father.

If those words make you want to drive to the airport and book a one-way flight to Rio, that's okay. You're not the first male of the species to be alarmed at the prospect and you certainly won't be the last. In fact, it might ease your mind to know that this author had a profound departure from reality when my wife told me she was pregnant five years ago.

First, I thought that there must be some mistake. I was 32 years old and just hitting my stride as a journalist in New York. What was I supposed to do with a baby? After I heard the news, I spent the next week wandering the city streets, wringing my hands, and talking to myself. How in the hell I was supposed to be a dad when I couldn't even balance my checkbook? Should I start acting stern and wearing black socks with my tennis shoes? What if the child doesn't like me? How in the heck do you change a diaper?

And yet, when I retrieved most of my senses, I began to realize that there's a reason pregnancy lasts nine months: it gives future fathers a chance to calm down and start learning how to be a dad.

Unfortunately, most baby books on the shelves when I was staring down the barrel of my future were written by moms for moms. Sure, there were dad chapters (never chapter one!), but the information was almost always about taking care of mom and filling in when she got tired. There was nothing out there about being a full-time dad who can't balance his checkbook.

Inside this book, which was written for men by a man, you'll not only find the answers to all your questions, you'll find a plan of action for the hard work ahead (and a few assurances that the decision you've made is what being a man is all about). Rest assured, there is a vast brotherhood of dads out there who stood in the same bewildered spot you're standing now, and we all made it through the first-year-spit-up-stained T-shirts and are all happier and wiser in the bargain. And don't worry; you *will* be able to go to Rio. You'll just have to pack an extra bag or two.

WHAT BEING A DAD IS ALL ABOUT

Being a dad has changed over the years. What used to be a pattern of "off to work early, home from work late" while Mom took care of the kids has now turned into "off to work early, home from work late after picking the kids up from day care because Mom has a job too and then helping get dinner on the table and the kids off to bed." At least that's the theory. Unfortunately most average working dads aren't picking up the pace as much as their now-professional female counterparts. We can do better, and better is what we should do.

Here's why. If we think back to our own childhoods (if we haven't completely suppressed those memories in our subconscious) , the one thing that we all have in common is we wish we could have spent more time with our own fathers. Now we as fathers have the opportunity to choose to spend more time with our kids. Being a dad still means providing for the family, but these days a growing number of employers are ever more aware of the demands put on both male and female parents, and in turn they are becoming more flexible. If dads spend more time at home with their children, then chances are the children will become more adjusted to life away from home. Plus, with not just one but two parents providing a nurturing, loving environment at home (previously, a Mom-only job), there can be a deeper level of trust between parents and kids, offering more self-confidence to kids when they're faced with challenges at school and in the playground.

Being a dad is a challenge (no one said it was going to easy). You will get a distinct lack of sleep for at least the first six months of your new baby's life. Nights out at the bar will become pleasant memories for a while. Even those casual and romantic evenings with your wife will be profoundly interrupted on a regular basis. And make no mistake, one of the challenges of being a new father is going to be finding the time to be romantic and alone with her—it's one of the keys to successful parenting.

You will have heard plenty of "never again" myths about life as a dad that fill you with horror. You will never have sex again, you will never ever be able to hang out with the guys again, you will never have a proper social life again, you will never travel again (unless it is in a minivan to go camping). Not sure about the others, but take it from me, the first one is definitely wrong. That's how we ended up with our second son. The truth is there are lots of changes and things to look forward to for future dads. Here are some of them:

SOME THINGS YOU CAN LOOK FORWARD TO

1. Changing your shirt on a more regular basis when baby is around.
2. Baby being around all the time . . . And I mean, *all* the time.
3. Learning to multitask (see page 6).
4. Watching infomercials at 3 a.m. on a regular basis.
5. Learning the difference between good baby poo and bad baby poo.
6. Turning the cushions on the sofa to hide stains.
7. Fathers' Day.

WHAT FUTURE DADS NEED TO KNOW ABOUT BONDING

For most dads, bonding isn't a problem. The first time they get a look at their baby's big, blue, round eyes, they're gonners—swept away with love at first sight and eager to hold, dress, rock, and bounce baby as much as if not more than Mom. But for other fathers, getting connected to their baby takes a while. They see their young one in their first couple of months as a cute kid, but one who only wants to sleep, eat, and cry all the time, not play football, talk politics, or read adventure stories. And who can blame those fathers? Infants do sleep all the time. They have been known to cry. And they do eat every two hours. That's just the way it is.

To those dads I would say that's okay. You're not the first dad to feel a little left out. But I would also say that there are some very simple things you can do to start getting to know your child and start forming that connection that will last for the rest of your life.

Simply putting baby in a front carrier and walking around the house is a type of bonding. As is giving baby a bath, or taking a nap with her. Any physical touch, smile, or 10-second stare in the eyes is all it takes—and that's not much.

By three months the baby will be smiling, laughing, and recognizing you. By six months you'll be able to make her smile just by being in the same room. And by one year, she'll be crawling or walking into your arms with delight. Before you know it, your baby won't be a baby anymore, but the bond you created by changing her diapers or holding her after a bad dream will last a lifetime.

YOU'RE HAVING A BABY!

In this chapter, you'll learn:

✻ Mom is the center of attention ✻ Your pregnant partner is going to look
and act a bit weird ✻ Ten things you can do to help your pregnant partner
✻ There's a thing called morning sickness for expectant fathers
✻ Sex during pregnancy might be a little different ✻ Birth classes aren't all bad
✻ How to prepare your home

LOGISTICS AND PREPARATIONS

Now that you have some idea of what being a dad is all about and you've decided to go for it, let's get to work. Remember: Pregnancy lasts nine months, which is a long time to get ready (both psychologically and physically) for the tiny new person you've invited to live with you in your house.

Dads should know that pregnancy and childbirth tend to be all about Mom, and she's the one who will be the center of attention these next nine months. It has nothing to do with how you smell or dress or the fact that you're male. That's just the way it is, and dads-to-be should just deal with that fact and recognize that they'll be in the background for a while. Your best bet is to not take offense and just to spend your time getting prepared. Also, now is a good time to start thinking about loading up on baby gear and carving out a spot in the house to put it all (and, eventually, the baby). Little boys and girls don't take up much room at first, but WOW! do they grow and acquire a lot of stuff.

CHANGES IN YOUR WOMAN

Before you jump ahead nine months to the day you bring home baby, future dads need to know one other thing: The women they're having a baby with is going to start acting—and looking—different.

I could say at this point that it's not your fault, that women's bodies undergo major hormonal shifts as they prepare for motherhood, but I won't lie to you. It is entirely your fault. That's why it's a good idea to arm yourself with knowledge, an extra dose of patience, and perhaps a 12-year-old single malt. You'll need at least the first two anyway when the baby comes.

If you haven't noticed by now, the first few months of pregnancy for a woman—the first trimester—are in many ways the hardest. Her body begins to prepare for taking care of not one but two beating hearts and not one but two appetites. In other words, your wife or girlfriend's body is working much harder than it normally does, even though she seems to be sitting on the couch a lot more often, drained of energy. That's because several things are happening inside her body, including an increase in hormones in the brain, a stretching of muscles in the uterus, a relaxing of muscles in the digestive tract, increased stomach acid, and a heightened sense of smell.

Oftentimes this all adds up to pre-menstrual-syndrome-like irritability and mood swings, fatigue, indigestion, gas, and vomiting. The vomiting part is known as morning sickness, but don't be fooled: the sickness can come at any time of the day. Morning sickness often goes away in the second trimester, though the indigestion and gas won't.

Things actually get back to a semblance of normality until the third trimester, when the large belly begins to take its toll on lower backs and hips, bringing on more fatigue as well as sleepless nights. During the last couple of weeks of pregnancy your partner becomes so huge and uncomfortable that if you even *think* about looking at a skinny blonde walking down the street, you'll get clobbered.

Well that's just super, you might be thinking. Just great. But let me tell you, this is an opportunity for us guys. By ratcheting up our patience and going that extra step more often than usual to help our partners in this time of queasy largeness, the rewards will be multiplied tenfold.

Also, it helps to remember that all this is going to be over soon. Your partner's roundness and emotional ups and downs might get replaced by harried fatigue and emotional ups and downs, but that will pass too as baby grows. Believe me, women don't like the extra weight of pregnancy either, which is why they'll first try to pin all the blame on you and then try to do something about it. As soon as they regain some strength after the baby is born, new moms are often anxious to get to the gym to work it all off. Until then, dads-to-be are encouraged to tread lightly and keep a level head about them even if their pregnant wives can't.

Following are a few small but effective activities a man can do to ensure lingering gratitude and, most importantly, lasting harmony with his pregnant partner.

TEN WAYS TO HELP YOUR PREGNANT PARTNER

1. Provide water and a toothbrush after vomiting.

2. Rub feet and calves at the end of the day.

3. Avoid the use of words "big," "huge," and "enormous."

4. Answer questions such as "Do you still find me attractive?" with an adamant "Of course I do!"

5. Replace the batteries in the remote.

6. Call from work a little more often.

7. Remind her gently that this was her idea too, not just yours.

8. Tell her in a convincing way that she looks pretty in those new pregnancy clothes.

9. Suggest that she take a long weekend (or two) at her mother's house.

10. Bring home flowers. Often.

MORNING SICKNESS FOR EXPECTANT FATHERS

It's been well documented that when their wives get pregnant and start eating for two (herself and the baby), men have a tendency to follow suit. In other words, if she needs a chocolate shake at 11 p.m. on a Tuesday, chances are you'll get one too. The same goes for that extra meal between lunch and dinner. In many cases, as grows Mommy, so grows Daddy. But let's just get this clear: You are eating just for one. There are no excuses.

Expectant dads may also mimic their partner's morning sickness and emotional frailty. Nausea, vomiting, indigestion, gas, mood swings, and fatigue—it's all a possibility. In a sign that future dads have at least some claim to the woes (and corresponding sympathy) of pregnancy, a group of scientists have given an official-sounding name to what affects men in the nine-month throws of anxiety leading up to fatherhood: couvade syndrome.

According to various studies done, couvade normally affects men in the third month and at the end of pregnancy. No one knows for sure why men start to feel like a bunch of pansies during this time, but some guesses include anxiety about becoming a father, jealousy that they're being left out of all the attention their partner is getting, and guilt for putting their partner in such a dire situation. In other words, it's just psychological. The cure usually includes getting more involved in the pregnancy and getting to know more about pregnancy and fatherhood by reading books like this one.

WHAT ABOUT SEX?

Contrary to popular myth, you know as well as I do that we don't want sex all the time. But, as you have already learned, pregnancy changes things. Because of the anxiety of becoming a father, not to mention the changes going on with their wife's body—specifically the expanding waistline, the indigestion, and the gas—guys can't be faulted for being a little less keen to jump in the sack as quickly as they did before the pregnancy. Some might even be afraid that they're going to hurt the baby (or Mommy) if they have sex during this time.

Then again, lots of men find their wife's fuller figure a turn-on, only to get the big turn-down more often than not. In that case, you can't blame a pregnant woman for not feeling entirely sexy if she thinks the contents of her stomach will end up in the toilet at a moment's notice. In short, sex during pregnancy tends to be a little more complicated.

That's why it's important to talk about it. At the very least, maybe you'll work each other into a lather, sending any anxiety out the window and throwing caution to the wind—just like old times! At best, though, you'll both be able to stay on the same page and stay connected through this challenging time. If you keep the communication lines very open during this time, you'll run less of a risk of being the cause of tears of frustration or of being thumped by an angry pregnant woman. Here are some things to keep in mind.

REMEMBER

1 Keep your sense of humor.

2 Sex during the first trimester may be the most difficult (with the exception of the last month) because of all the nausea and discomfort your partner is feeling.

3 Sex during the last two months might just be too difficult because of the extra-large size of your partner.

4 You cannot damage the baby; he or she is very well insulated inside the uterus and the amniotic sac.

5 The baby will not be "scarred for life"—he or she can't see what you're doing and even if he or she could, they'd have no idea whatsoever what was going on. If you have niggling worries, ask your doctor for their advice.

6 Sexual positions that you enjoyed before or in the early stages of pregnancy can be uncomfortable or even unsafe at later stages of the baby's development. For example, a woman should avoid lying flat on her back after the first trimester, because the weight of the growing uterus puts pressure on major blood vessels. Many pregnant women enjoy sex in positions where they are lying sideways or where they are on top.

7 Sex and orgasm can trigger contractions, though the chances that it will bring on early labor are slim. This has, however, been known to be a good way to encourage labor if a woman is past her due date.

8 Sex is still about the most fun you can have with your clothes off (or on).

PRENATAL CLASSES

For most first-time dads (and almost all second-time dads), attending prenatal classes is not how they would choose to spend a Saturday afternoon. After all, we men can't be blamed for feeling a bit funny sitting in a room full of strangers talking about a woman's discharges, mood swings, and engorged breasts while watching grainy videos of unknown women giving birth.

Even so, there are a number of good reasons to attend these classes, if only because after taking them you'll feel more involved in what's going on and less out of the loop. Plus, when the birth day does arrive you won't look too lost and worthless when your partner starts screaming, "It hurts!"

LAMAZE, BRADLEY, AND YOU

In addition to helping dads feel more connected to the pregnancy (as well as less anxious about what will happen), prenatal classes are also great places to meet and commiserate with other first-time parents. Seeing how utterly petrified someone else is can be a great way to allay your own fears. Mostly, though, prenatal classes offer concrete, useable advice and instructions on what to do on the day the baby decides to come on out.

When you take a class you can expect to find up to a dozen other couples all sitting or lying on the floor (you'll soon join them), while an instructor who is almost always female explains what to do when contractions start. You'll learn a lot about the biological aspects of giving birth, including what a contraction is (the muscles of the uterus contracting) and how to time them. Most of the class deals with how to help your partner make it through childbirth with the least amount of pain and the most comfort. The two most widely attended types of classes are named after the method of childbirth most widely practiced: Lamaze and Bradley.

LAMAZE

This may be the best-known type of prenatal class and is offered through most hospitals and care providers throughout the world. The method was ushered into the mainstream in the 1950s by the French obstetrician Dr. Ferdinand Lamaze. He thought that by breathing and relaxing through each contraction and by visualizing what's going on inside her body, the pregnant woman could minimize the pain of childbirth.

When you take a Lamaze class you'll learn these techniques, as well as a long list of other things to do with labor and the first few days and weeks after baby comes. For expectant dads, there is a lot of practice about how to be a good coach during labor. Both of you will learn how to communicate as effectively as possible during the process of labor and what to expect when you get to the hospital. You'll also get to ask questions about technical procedures such as the epidural shot or Caesarian section.

Classes are usually spaced out over about six weeks, though you can take the crash course over the weekend, if you've got the stamina.

BRADLEY

The Bradley Method (also known by the catchy title of Husband-Coached Childbirth) was started in the 1940s by Dr. Robert Bradley. It emphasizes totally natural birth with no drugs during labor. Good diet and exercise during pregnancy is part of the method, in addition to pain management through deep-relaxation techniques and visualization exercises.

Expectant dads also play a large role during labor for those who choose the Bradley Method. You'll learn some very pointed things to say to help your wife or girlfriend relax when a contraction comes. The idea for the woman is to think her way through each contraction by actively relaxing every part of her body and allowing her uterus to do the work it was made to do at this point (i.e. push the baby out). This method teaches the mom-to-be how to emulate a "sleep-breathing" technique, which is supposed to relax her as much as humanly possible.

The classes last between eight and 12 hours, spread out over around 12 weeks. Course instructors also suggest a lot of practice at home, to develop your coaching skills in the lead-up to the big day.

YOU

Maybe you don't dig Lamaze; perhaps you'd like to tell Bradley where to shove it. But without throwing the baby out with the bathwater (sorry, an inexcusable pun), now is the time to do some pre-birth prep and for you and your wife to decide how you'd like to play it when the labor starts. That means talking through all your fears and expectations about the birth and practicing your back-rubbing skills. Following are some other preparation activities for your own sanity.

MENTAL PREP PRE-BIRTH CHECKLIST FOR DAD

☑ Sleep late on weekends and revel in the fact that no one needs you to get up right this instant.

☑ Take a vacation with your wife to a foreign country. Enjoy the light luggage and the inflight martinis.

☑ Spend time indulging in any of your favorite childhood activities. Build a model airplane, dig out your favorite children's storybooks, rediscover your dusty trumpet. You won't quite get to return to childhood when baby is born, but remembering the fun of it all helps.

☑ Watch a film, read a book, listen to a CD from start to finish. Uninterrupted. Pure joy.

☑ A father is a man with photos in his wallet where money used to be. Enjoy your last chance to spend money guilt-free.

☑ In the last weeks of pregnancy, stock your shelves and fridge with easy-to-make food and drink (yes, beer is considered "easy to make").

HOW TO PREPARE YOUR HOME

Some people go crazy decorating a nursery for their first child, painting the room pink or blue and loading up with cute boyish or girly items hung about the room like a carnival gift shop. (Second children, by the way, are lucky to get a pink or blue doll, much less a whole room painted in that color.) But before you load up on the cute stuff, know first of all that you don't actually *need* most of that stuff, but that there are a few items you absolutely must have to host a new baby. These are the things that will really help you bring up a baby even when the stuffed gorilla doll has split its seams and lost its stuffing.

Also, know that most likely baby is going to be sleeping in your room (and possibly your bed) for at least the first three months. Luckily the young one can't crawl or walk just yet, so you don't have to worry about your CD collection or all the electrical outlets at baby level. That worry will come later. Right now, it's advisable to set aside a dark, quiet room (if you have one) or corner of the house where baby can sleep and Daddy can go to decompress.

Following are the key items you'll need to make way for a new member of your family. Think about asking friends whose babies have grown into lovable toddlers whether you might be able to inherit some of their baby equipment. It doesn't all have to be new or the flashiest brand name, but it does have to be certified as having met safety standards and, most of all, it has to be practical and Dad-friendly.

KEY EQUIPMENT

- ☑ Bassinet
- ☑ Crib
- ☑ Changing table or diaper-changing station
- ☑ Diaper pail
- ☑ Washing machine and dryer
- ☑ Baby clothes
- ☑ Washable cotton rags (for spit-up and other stuff)
- ☑ Soft blankets and other cuddly, warm things to wrap baby in
- ☑ New dresser to keep all baby's new clothes, spit-up rags, cuddly blankets, etc.
- ☑ Rocking chair or glider
- ☑ Baby carrier (over-the-shoulder slings are cool these days)
- ☑ Baby carriage
- ☑ Car seat

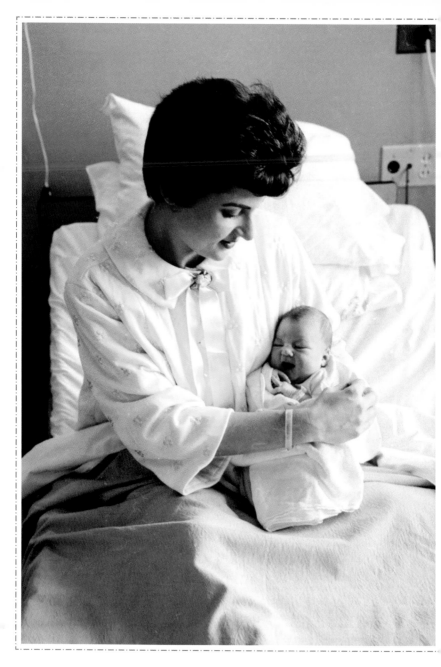

LIFE WILL NEVER BE THE SAME

In this chapter, you'll learn:

✽ How to stay calm ✽ What to bring
✽ How to help get that baby out ✽ What (not) to say
and do during the stages of labor ✽ How to time contractions
✽ When not to go out with the guys

THIS IS IT!

You've made it through the morning sickness, the gas, and the sleepless, uncomfortable nights with your relationship intact. The house is in order and you've bought, constructed, and installed all the baby gear. Your wife or girlfriend is huge and over it. Then, in the middle of the night she'll start to feel a mild contraction. This is it! That baby ain't paying rent, so it's time to get it out, out, out!

What you *don't* want to do when your wife tells you the baby's coming is turn white with shock, run around in a panic with your hands in the air, or call an emergency hotline. None of that is helpful. She's the one who's about to have a baby. You're the one who needs to be the calm voice of reason and the steady ship in the storm. You also need to be the family-appointed security detail. In the coming hours, there will be in-laws, nurses, midwives, hospital administrators, neighbors, and others who want to annoy your wife, stress her out, and cause labor to last an eternity. It's your job to screen them and keep all non-essential personnel behind a previously established perimeter.

In addition to staying calm and taking charge, you can also help by driving swiftly but safely to the hospital, if that's where you're having the baby. If you're having a home birth, do not drive to the hospital. Helping also includes carrying a previously packed suitcase, saying positive and encouraging words, and generally being kind and supportive. Oh and if your wife calls to tell you she's having a baby while you're at the bar with your friends, don't have another beer before you leave. Don't even finish the beer you are currently working on. Just leave.

THE HOSPITAL BAG

Well before you're wife goes into labor, she will have packed a small suitcase with extra clothes, perfumes, toiletries and, yes, diapers and baby clothes. Future dads should think about bringing along a few things too. First births can last a long time, so be prepared. Following is a list of ideas to consider.

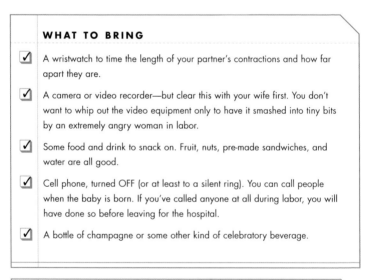

WHAT TO BRING

- ✓ A wristwatch to time the length of your partner's contractions and how far apart they are.

- ✓ A camera or video recorder—but clear this with your wife first. You don't want to whip out the video equipment only to have it smashed into tiny bits by an extremely angry woman in labor.

- ✓ Some food and drink to snack on. Fruit, nuts, pre-made sandwiches, and water are all good.

- ✓ Cell phone, turned OFF (or at least to a silent ring). You can call people when the baby is born. If you've called anyone at all during labor, you will have done so before leaving for the hospital.

- ✓ A bottle of champagne or some other kind of celebratory beverage.

WHAT NOT TO BRING

- ✗ Hand-held video games
- ✗ iPod or CD player
- ✗ Television
- ✗ Work
- ✗ Your buddies

HOW TO BE A REAL MAN

Saying and doing the right things during labor is your key performance goal—your entire job description. You, more than any other person, will be the anchor in your partner's stormy seas. It is you she will look to for confidence and guidance when she feels like she can't go through another contraction or when it's time to push the baby out. Even women who get pain medication and a Caesarean operation need someone to allay their fears. As their partner in this momentous journey that started nine months ago, you're the one who can ease the fears and provide that needed boost of assurance. Sometimes saying nothing whatsoever and just holding her hand and looking into her eyes is the best help of all.

To know exactly what to say and do, it helps first to inform yourself as to exactly what happens during labor and delivery. There are three stages of having a baby: the first stage is labor, which includes early, active, and transitional phases; the second stage is pushing and delivery; and the third stage is pushing out the placenta.

Usually, though, labor will be as action-packed for you as it is for your partner. Massaging the lower back and feet, wiping her brow with a cool, damp cloth, breathing along with her are all helpful things to know how to do. Even if your wife doesn't want you to touch her at all (which, she might say, is what got her into this mess in the first place!), you'll be keeping friends and family at bay, running for ice chips and water, and making sure the nurses and doctors don't try to give your wife any unneeded shots or try to push her prematurely to get a Caesarean.

THE FIRST STAGE OF LABOR: WHAT TO SAY AND DO

This first stage starts when your partner begins to feel the first twinge of contractions and it lasts all the way up until it's time to push the baby out. What's happening is the large bag of muscles known as the uterus is pulling open the cervix (this process is also known as "dilating") so that the baby can come down the vaginal canal. The stage starts out calm enough, but as your partner's cervix opens more and more, the contractions get more intense and more painful. The jargon you need to know is "early," "active phase," and "transition."

In the early labor, contractions will last between 30 and 45 seconds and can be up to 20 minutes apart, though most likely they'll be about 10 minutes apart. In the active second phase of the first stage of labor, contractions will get stronger and will last 40 to 60 seconds and be 3 to 4 minutes apart. During transition, the cervix dilates from 7 to 10 centimeters—this is the last and most intense time before pushing. Contractions come in waves and last 60 to 90 seconds. Sometimes

Phases		LENGTH OF CONTRACTIONS
Early labor	1	Contractions last 30–45 seconds and are up to 20 minutes apart
Active Phase	2	Contractions last 40–60 seconds and are 3–4 minutes apart
Transition	3	Contractions come in waves and last 60–90 seconds—they can feel as though there is no break or they can be up to 2 minutes apart

these contractions can be about 2 minutes apart, but many women say it feels as though there is no break between them.

Now that the basics are out of the way, you'll have a better idea of your role. You are the coach and it's your job to get your wife and your new baby across the finish line.

You will need	STEPS
A firm constitution **Patience** **A watch** **A sense of humor** **Food** **A few good, strong words**	**1** Using a watch with a second counter, time the duration of each contraction and how far apart they are. Write this information down in list form on a blank sheet of paper. This will inform you both and give you both the feeling that you're in charge and under control (at least until you get to the hospital). The length of time between contractions should be timed from the beginning of one contraction to the beginning of the next. Note that it is not a measure of time between the end of one and the beginning of another. **2** From the early labor to transition, always give your wife reassuring words such as "You can do it," "This is what we've been waiting for," "Breathe through it," "The baby will be here soon," and "Go, man, go" (if appropriate). **3** Stay calm and relaxed. If you can't remain calm then fake it. If you start trying to talk to your wife and you have a look of horror on your face, then she's going to freak out too and you will have a very long night. (continued on next page)

S T E P S (continued)

4 Try to eat something to keep your energy up, but don't stuff in a meatball sandwich right in front of your laboring wife. If she doesn't get sick at the sight of it, she'll likely remind you to get that *#!@ thing out of her face.

5 Keep the door to the labor room closed and be very mindful of who is coming in and what they want. Even well-meaning sisters can stress out a laboring woman, and stress will only prevent the uterus from doing its job. In fact, when a woman "fights" contractions because they hurt or because she's tense, the contractions are going to hurt worse and the labor is going to take longer. Total relaxation is going to be your wife's best friend, and you can help tremendously by promoting calmness from start to finish. That way the body can take its natural course with as few distractions as possible.

6 Look for stressed-out body parts—wrinkled forehead, tense shoulders, arched feet, clenched fists—and remind your partner to relax them.

7 After each difficult contraction, remind your partner to rest and relax until the next one. When they start coming in waves during transition, start telling her to ride the wave to its crest and then down the other side.

8 Say more encouraging words, unless she doesn't want to hear anything. Use as few words as possible during the latter stages of labor; many men have discovered that small talk or babbling during transition is met with hostility.

9 Massage feet, the lower back, the abdomen, or any place that feels good to your partner. She'll let you know if something doesn't feel good—believe me on this one.

THE SECOND STAGE OF LABOR: WHAT TO SAY AND DO

When your partner begins to feel an intense urge to push the baby out, that's the sign that the cervix is fully dilated and it's ready to start the second stage of labor: delivery. This is a crucial time and all most dads can do is hold hands with their partner (or just stand nearby), offer encouraging words (or none at all), and look on with a combination of newfound respect and unbelieving horror.

You will need		STEPS
A firmer constitution	1	Continue to give words of encouragement, especially when she's pushing through a contraction. If she begins to doubt her ability to push the baby out, say things like, "You can do it," "Our baby is almost here," and "Push the pain out."
	2	Do whatever might help your partner. If you don't know what these are by now, she'll definitely let you know. This might include going away altogether and leaving her to it. Don't be offended, just go with it.
	3	Remind her to breathe through the pain and breathe with her, using the techniques you learned in a prenatal class. If you didn't take a prenatal class, just know that you shouldn't breathe too fast—it might cause hyperventilation.

(continued on next page)

S T E P S (continued)

The general idea is that the breathing gets deeper and faster as the labor progresses. You might also have learned in prenatal classes about helping your wife pick a focal point and to concentrate on this during each contraction. Now is the time to bring out any dormant coaching skills.

4 If you're in a hospital delivery room and your wife is wearing a fetal monitor, ask the doctors how to read it so you can give your wife updates.

5 When you can see the baby's head crowning, guide your wife's hand down to touch it and say more encouraging words like, "It's almost here!," "You're doing great! or "Just a little bit more!" Do not say things like "Eeew, gross!" or "It's an alien!" This will not help things.

6 When the baby comes out, try not to blubber and weep too much, especially if your wife is as cool as a cucumber. Then again, why not? You've been the stoic sentry fending off family members for hours, or even days. It may be time to let it all out.

7 Your final action is to cut the umbilical cord. But don't just grab any sharp instrument you see. Wait until the doctor or midwife has tied it off and given you the go-ahead and a pair of surgical scissors. Also, know that the cord isn't as delicate as it looks and is more like a tough piece of meat gristle. You'll have to put some real effort into it.

THE THIRD STAGE OF LABOR: WHAT TO SAY AND DO

If you've managed not to have flopped on the floor in a heap of tears or a queasy lump of nausea during delivery, then you're a stronger man than I. Either that or you have some pent-up childhood emotional scars and you need therapy. Regardless, the baby has arrived and everyone should feel a sense of relief and euphoria. The only thing left to do is for your wife to push out the placenta, which was attached to the inside of her uterus and served, via the umbilical cord, as your baby's life support system for the past nine months. The process of delivering the placenta shouldn't take long at all—say 10 or 15 minutes.

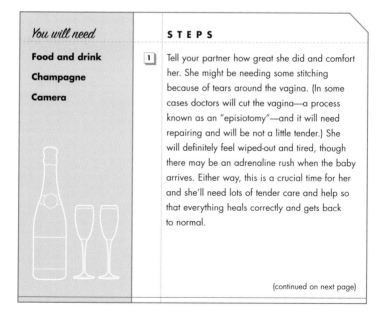

You will need	STEPS
Food and drink **Champagne** **Camera**	**1** Tell your partner how great she did and comfort her. She might be needing some stitching because of tears around the vagina. (In some cases doctors will cut the vagina—a process known as an "episiotomy"—and it will need repairing and will be not a little tender.) She will definitely feel wiped-out and tired, though there may be an adrenaline rush when the baby arrives. Either way, this is a crucial time for her and she'll need lots of tender care and help so that everything heals correctly and gets back to normal.

(continued on next page)

S T E P S (continued)

2 Break out something to drink for your partner. She's likely thirsty as hell. Now's not a bad time to eat either. After our first son was born, my wife and I sent a friend out for cheeseburgers, which we gladly ate not an hour after the birth.

3 Do not say things like, "The baby is so ugly," "Check out his mammoth cone head," or "He looks like your old boyfriend."

4 Get in some initial dad bonding time by holding your little one and marveling at the fact that you helped bring about the existence of this adorable (if wrinkly) tiny bundle.

5 Hear the sound of your baby's crying and get used to it.

6 Snap some first photos of the newborn and new mom, though screen the pictures afterwards—oftentimes the photos taken during the excitement of the delivery room are not the most flattering. It's not a wise idea to upload these to the hospital's "new baby" website or send them out on a blanket email. Have some reserve.

7 Open the champagne and have a toast with anyone you can find (except the baby).

8 Practice saying the words "Mom" and "Dad" and "daughter" or "son" in reference to the new roles in your new family.

WHEN NOT TO GO OUT WITH THE GUYS

You may have started on the bubbly in the delivery room, but that doesn't mean you should keep on drinking in celebration far into the night with your friends. In fact, it would be wise to turn down any invitations to carouse at the bar with your pals for the next couple of weeks at least—or until a routine is established at home. You'll lose big points with your partner if you fail to heed this advice. You may get some time off if your mother-in-law comes to stay, however. Strange to say, you will soon be thinking differently about having her visit.

DON'T GO OUT WHEN ...

☒ The baby is "crying too much."

☒ Your wife or girlfriend refuses to get out of bed, appears depressed and harried, and has taken to sharpening the kitchen knives more than once a day.

☒ Your mates tell you you're wimping out for being such a domestic. Keep in mind they have no idea what it's like a) being in a committed relationship and b) being a contributor to the miracle of procreation.

☒ It's the baby's one-week, one-month, three-month, six-month, and one-year birthdays (and really, any major event after that!).

☒ Your wife or girlfriend asks you not to.

☒ Your wife and new baby lie down for a short nap (you should take one too).

☒ Your eyes keep closing involuntarily.

KEEPING
BABY SAFE

In this chapter, you'll learn:

✻ The football hold ✻ The forward-facing chair hold
✻ How to wear a sling with pride ✻ How to baby-proof the home
✻ How to travel with baby

A HIGH-MAINTENANCE
NEW ROOMMATE

Now that the baby is safely out of Mommy and into the house, it's important that you learn how to be safe when you do get home. That involves a few modifications, but also some learning on your part. For example, don't leave baby on the edge of a table or bed—little ones, even newborns, like to wriggle and roll. There are also some things to know about driving around with an infant in the car. Plus, if you didn't know before how to hold a baby, now's the time to learn. From here on out, you have a new high-maintenance roommate who needs a lot of looking after.

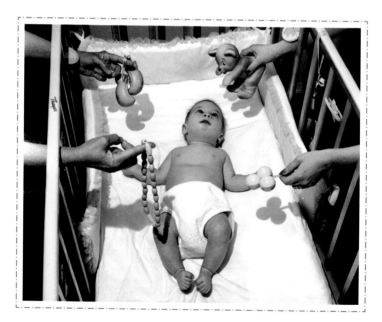

HOW TO HOLD BABY

This is important. For one, Mom isn't going to want to lug the baby around all the time. Second, it's actually quite nice to gather your tiny bundle of joy up in your arms and do a little bonding. In fact, research has shown that babies who are held most of the time get so much of their need for human contact and touch met early on that they cry less and become more independent, confident, and happy as toddlers and into later years.

That said, holding an infant can be nerve-wracking, especially for men who aren't used to being overly tender. You might have shied away from holding babies before when friends or relatives thrust their "adorable" infants into your arms. Lots of guys simply worry they're going to hurt baby by holding too hard or dropping the poor little bundle. The crying doesn't help sooth nerves either.

Happily, there are several different techniques for holding a baby, including the traditional cradle hold, the stomach hold, the shoulder hold, the football hold, and my favorite, the forward-facing chair hold. You can also get yourself a sling or a baby carrier for those times you need both hands for a little home repair.

The one constant with any "hold" is that you absolutely must support baby's head and neck; until about six months an infant's neck muscles are not strong enough to hold its own head up. Also, be aware that babies—even the youngest ones—can push off and flop around quite a bit as they test out their forming muscles. You don't want to hold babies too tight, but you don't want them pushing off and out of your arms either.

CRADLE HOLD

This is one of the easiest ways to hold a baby. Simply rest the baby's head in the inner bend of one arm with your forearm extending under his or her back and your hand on baby's lower back or bottom. Your other arm should run parallel to the first so that your hand can help support the baby's head.

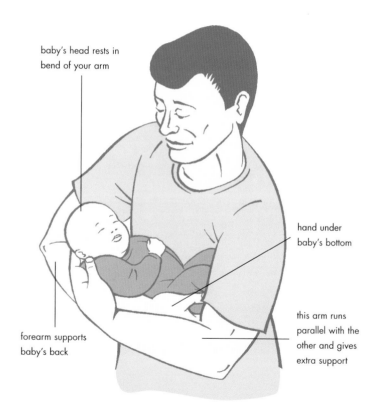

baby's head rests in bend of your arm

hand under baby's bottom

forearm supports baby's back

this arm runs parallel with the other and gives extra support

STOMACH HOLD

For babies with excessive gas, being held stomach-down can be a relief. Simply slide one arm under baby's tummy and rest his or her head in the palm of your hand. Baby's legs and arms should hang down on either side of your arm. Bring your arm close to your stomach to help support him or her and use your other arm for extra stability.

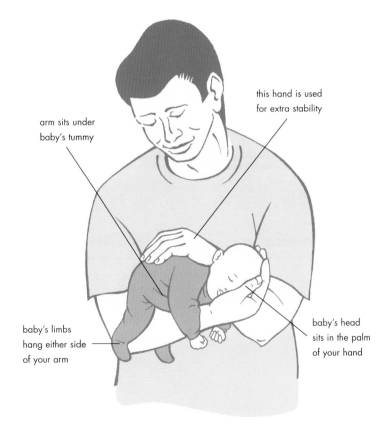

this hand is used for extra stability

arm sits under baby's tummy

baby's limbs hang either side of your arm

baby's head sits in the palm of your hand

SHOULDER HOLD

A key hold for burping babies as well as a pretty comfortable hold, the shoulder hold is one every dad should learn. Just wrap one arm under baby's bottom while his or her stomach or chest rests against your chest and shoulder. Place your free hand on baby's back for support.

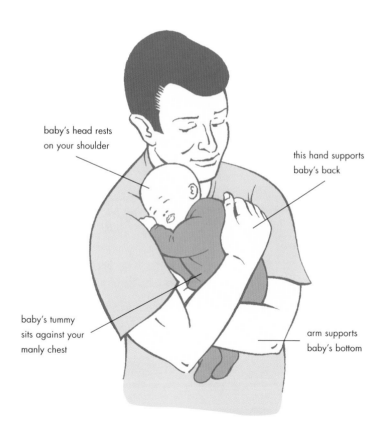

baby's head rests on your shoulder

this hand supports baby's back

baby's tummy sits against your manly chest

arm supports baby's bottom

FOOTBALL HOLD

Just like a football player tucks the ball under his arm as he runs down the field, you can tuck your baby under your arm (though you might not want to do any running). The baby will lie on their back along the length of one arm with their head in your hand and feet extending toward your back. This hold is best used by Mom while breastfeeding, but that doesn't mean you can't give it the old college try yourself.

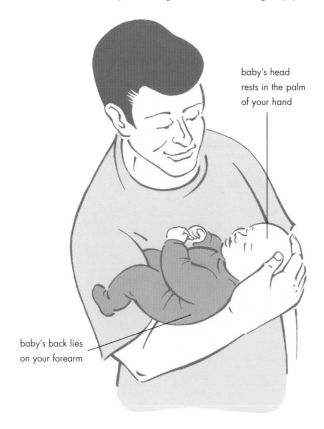

baby's head rests in the palm of your hand

baby's back lies on your forearm

FORWARD-FACING CHAIR HOLD

I call this one the chair hold because you use one hand to support the baby's bottom or legs while he or she leans back against your chest and shoulder as if sitting in a chair. Your free hand should be placed on the baby's stomach or chest to help support him or her and to keep baby from flopping forward. This is a great hold when you're sitting down. It takes some practice to feel confident for long periods of standing up.

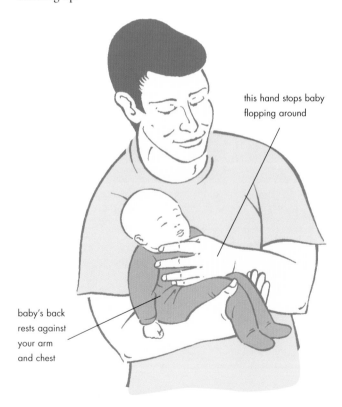

this hand stops baby flopping around

baby's back rests against your arm and chest

SLINGS AND BABY CARRIERS

After about two months of carrying baby around, you might start to feel a twinge in your lower back and shoulders—babies are small but they reach 15 pounds quickly. You also might want to free up at least one arm to actually get something done while baby is awake and ready to play. In that case, get yourself a baby sling that goes over one shoulder or buy a front baby carrier that straps over your shoulder and back. You might think you look silly with one of these things on—and you do. Just get used to it. You're a dad now.

happy baby

this might not look cool but it leaves your hands free

SAFETY IN THE HOME

When baby is brand new—say up to six months old—you don't have to worry about him or her sticking a stray chopstick in the wall plug. For one, they can't crawl or walk, and for two, where the hell are they going to find a chopstick? What you do have to worry about is making sure that baby will be secure in the places he spends most of his time, such as a crib and a changing table. It's when he starts crawling and walking that you'll want to break out the plug protectors and hide the poison. Following is a checklist of precautions to take.

SAFETY IN THE HOME: ZERO TO SIX MONTHS

☑ First off, make sure you've constructed the crib and changing table correctly and securely. Don't risk the furniture collapsing while the baby is in or on it.

☑ If you have a changing table, make sure it has some kind of edge protection or strap-down belt built in so that baby can't roll off onto the floor. If you don't have anything to keep baby from rolling off, just make sure never to leave him unattended. In fact, even if you do have protections in place, don't leave the baby unattended.

☑ Should you take the above precautions and the baby still rolls off and takes a fall, you will have been wise to put a plush rug down to cushion the impact.

☑ In an infant's crib, it's important not to fill it with anything soft and cuddly. Babies can suffocate on fluffy blankets, pillows, over-soft mattresses, stuffed animals, and the like.

☑ Make sure the slats on the crib are close enough together so that baby doesn't get his head stuck between them. This could be an issue for old cribs.

SAFETY IN THE HOME: SIX MONTHS TO A YEAR

☑ Place plastic plug outlet protections in each and every plug around the house. You may find it annoying to have to pull these things out when you want to plug in the vacuum cleaner, but it's worth it. Besides, most everything won't be as easy as it used to be now that you're a parent.

☑ Put cabinet locks on all cabinets so that small hands can't get to what's inside, like the cleaning products. Even with cabinet locks it's a good idea to put any toxic cleaners or spare poison into locked upper cabinets, just in case.

☑ Consider padding all sharp corners (coffee tables, brick fireplaces, etc.). You won't win any interior design awards, but your infant will avoid regular dangerous prangs.

☑ Place safety gates or barriers at the top and bottom of stairs.

☑ Never leave small objects or plastic bags, which can cause choking, within baby's reach.

☑ Don't put baby down alone on a waterbed, beanbag, or soft blanket that could cover his face and cause suffocation.

☑ Make sure you use the harness properly every time you put baby in a highchair.

☑ Set the temperature of your hot water system to 120°F to prevent accidental scalding.

☑ Put down some nonskid backing on any slippery rugs.

☑ Remove tall precarious stacks of CDs, if not because they'll fall over on tiny heads, because it's no fun having to reorganize your music collection.

☑ Be careful of houseplants low to the ground. Toddlers have been known to gobble the greenery, and you never know what's poisonous or not.

FOOD SAFETY

At first there's not much dads need to worry about when it comes to food for baby, especially if Mom and her breasts are breakfast, lunch, and dinner for the little one. Even if you're feeding baby formula, there's really not much to worry about in the choking department. It's when babies start eating solids—anywhere from four to six months—that you have to be vigilant. That's when everything, not just food, starts to go in the mouth.

TEN FOODS THAT CHOKE

1. Large chunks of meat
2. Grapes
3. Whole berries
4. Small, raw carrots
5. Apple slices
6. Dry cereal
7. Potato chips
8. Popcorn
9. Nuts
10. Hard candy

The food that does go into your young baby's mouth should be limited to rice cereal, puréed vegetables and puréed fruit for at least the first nine months. After that, make sure all food is soft and is cut into very small, baby-mouthful pieces. You might find that baby doesn't so much as chew as suck her solids down, so think about the sorts of food her tiny mouth and body can cope with. Also, don't let baby pull up, crawl, or bounce up and down in her highchair while she's eating. This sort of behavior always presents the risk of lodging food morsels in windpipes—not where food should go.

FOODS TO AVOID BEFORE 12 MONTHS

[X] Any foods with high levels of nitrates, which can cause anemia. These include beets, turnips, collard greens, and spinach.

[X] Honey: It can cause botulism in children whose immune systems have not yet been fortified enough to ward off such things.

[X] Any foods that have been treated with pesticides, hormones, antibiotics, or other chemicals. Organic may be the best way to go for babies.

OTHER FOODS TO AVOID IN THE FIRST YEAR

In addition to preventing choking, dads should be aware that baby can't eat just anything, even if they've made the switch to solid food. Also, be aware of how you're keeping foods between meals: breast milk or formula in a bottle that has been partially eaten should not be reused under any circumstances. Also, make sure you wash your hands before preparing any food, especially after having changed baby's diaper.

SAFETY IN THE CAR

Unlike 35 years ago, when children were allowed to roam freely inside cars with or without seatbelts on, nowadays there are car seats and a host of rules that go with them. And this is a good thing. Car seats are sturdy and designed to save lives if you were to get into an accident. Remember that the seatbelts that come with your car are designed for adults and are not good enough to keep your child safe. It won't be until baby has grown to a strapping 4 foot 9 inches and 80 pounds that you can use just a regular seatbelt. On the opposite page is a list of guidelines to consider when outfitting your youngster with the right seat.

Don't drive around without baby strapped into her seat, even if you're just popping down to the corner store. It's just not smart. You could get baby seriously injured and get yourself arrested for negligence. Also, just remember that when you're driving with a baby, you're going to stop a lot to feed and change diapers, and that's going to add time to your trip. Again, planning will help make your trip far more stress- and frustration-free. You might also get to places on time.

INSTALLING A CAR SEAT

There are varying rules and regulations when it comes to securing a car seat before buckling your child in, but some general rules apply everywhere. Also, each car seat is going to come with a set of detailed instructions. Read and follow them to the letter.

CAR SEAT POINTERS

- ✓ Infants and toddlers under 20 pounds should face toward the back of the car, which is far safer than facing the front.

- ✓ Many car seats have built-in levels so you can ensure the seat isn't leaning too far forward or back, which is also important if you're in an accident. However, if your baby's head keeps flopping forward when she goes to sleep in the car, it's okay to tilt the seat back slightly more. You can do this by putting a folded-up towel under the front part of the seat.

- ✓ Try to get a safe car seat that has a base and a removable seat that you can pop in and out when baby is asleep. It's amazingly helpful, as strapping car seats in with seatbelts is a true pain in the ass.

- ✓ All kids under about 40 pounds should have a three-point harness seatbelt. After that they can go to car booster seats and use the car's over-the-shoulder seatbelt.

- ✓ The middle of the back seat is always the safest place to put a car seat.

- ✓ Make sure the base of the seat is flat. Thread the seatbelt through and buckle it. (Read the instructions that come with the car seat to find out exactly where you need to put the belt—all seats are different.)

- ✓ Pull the shoulder belt tight to check that it locks. If the seatbelts in your car aren't the locking kind, invest in a locking clip that fits onto the car seatbelt just over the buckle.

- ✓ Many car seats now come with tether systems, which consist of a belt that secures the seat to a permanent metal anchor welded to the frame of the car. Usually tether anchors can be found on the floor board in front of the back seat or on the rear dash behind the seat. These are used instead of the car seatbelts.

HOW TO TRAVEL WITH BABY

Traveling with babies younger than one year old can be both enlightening and harrowing, and a lot of it has to do with the method of travel. Walking with baby in a carrier is a pleasant bonding experience for Dad and baby most of the time, though a soiled diaper might put a kink in this plan, as would a bad back on Dad's part. In those cases, changing baby's diaper while walking baby around in a stroller or buggy might be a better prospect. Plus, babies love to sit up, get pushed around, and look at everything. Who wouldn't?

THE DO'S AND DON'TS OF DRIVING WITH BABY

[X] Don't think that you can make it in the car for more than two hours without stopping.

[X] Don't drive faster so that you can make it to your destination before baby wakes up.

[✓] Do learn to love nursery rhymes played over and over and over.

[✓] Do learn to drive safely even when your baby's screams are piercing your innermost being.

[X] Don't drive with one hand while using the other to play with baby in the back seat.

[X] Don't curse, yell at other drivers, or otherwise succumb to road rage. You're a dad now. You have standards, man.

[X] Don't fall asleep because you were up with the baby all night.

[X] Don't fall asleep because you were out with the guys all night.

[X] Don't get a flat tire.

As for car travel, some babies love it and some don't. When they don't, driving is a mightily stressful thing. Imagine being stuck in traffic while baby is screaming bloody murder from the back seat. Not fun. Not fun at all. Flying with baby and without Mom is not recommended—but if you have to do it, you have to do it.

Any way you choose to transport baby, just make sure you take along diapers, baby wipes, and a blanket. Longer trips, if you've never taken one with a tiny baby, require an astonishing amount of stuff, even if it's just an overnighter. You have to bring blankets, spit-up rags, favorite stuffed animals, toys, a portable crib (if you feel uncomfortable letting baby sleep with you in the same bed), bottles, sterilizers, powders, ointments, and a thousand changes of clothes. Makes you realize why families buy station wagons.

TRAVEL BY PLANE

We've all been on a crowded plane with a baby who won't stop crying, and we've all imagined stuffing that baby and his good-for-nothing father in the plane's bathroom and locking the door. And that's the nice version. Well, that was before we had kids. Now that you're a dad and you're flying, the tables have turned. It's you who will be held responsible for any crying, and it's your baby that every passenger who gets on the plane will stare at with dread. Luckily not all babies cry and squeal on airplanes. Many just sleep through the whole experience as if they were at home. To make sure you're one of the lucky ones, take some precautions.

Unfortunately, lots of people who fly have never had kids themselves. That's why the airplane passengers who glare and shake their heads at you when your baby is upset don't know (and don't care) that babies cry for a reason. Chances are if your baby is crying he's hungry, he has a wet diaper, or he's in some discomfort, which on airplanes is likely to come from the altitude change and the pressure it exerts on tiny ears. That's why it's essential to get baby to suck on something—preferably Mom's breast—while taking off and landing. This will allow their ears to "pop" (i.e. it equalizes the pressure inside the ear with that of the outside the eardrum), thereby relieving the most common and the most painful reason for baby's tears. Now you just have to contend with the cramped quarters, the inability to lie down, and the stress of boarding and getting off.

HOW TO FLY SUCCESSFULLY WITH A BABY

- [✓] Avoid busy times of year.
- [✓] Stroll your baby to the gate, at which point the crew will check your buggy for the flight, handing it back to you when you land.
- [✓] Try to get a seat as close to the front as possible.
- [✓] Befriend a doting stranger who looks like they would love to hold baby for the Bangkok to New York stretch.
- [✓] Reconsider flying with sick babies or babies with hay fever—congestion can block ear canals and make it impossible for baby's ears to equalize.
- [✗] Don't bring a lot of carry-on luggage that you have to juggle along with a baby.
- [✓] Bring extra pacifiers, bottles, or whatever else you think baby will suck on successfully.
- [✓] Accept any help crew members wish to bestow.
- [✓] Bring a warm, comfy blanket—flights are often cold.
- [✓] Keep your cool—your baby will know when you don't.

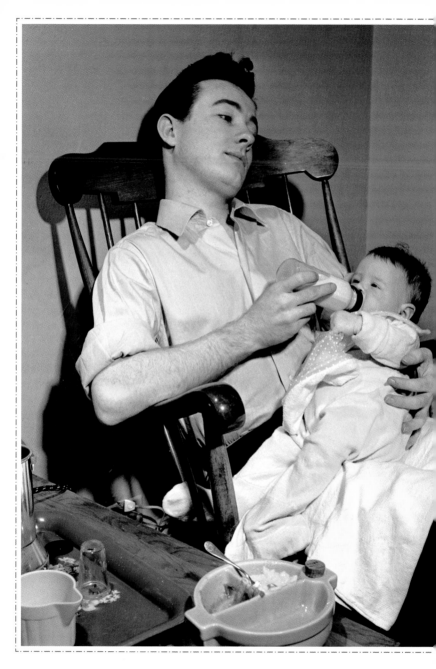

SOME
IMPORTANT
BASICS

Babycare 101

In this chapter, you'll learn:

✻ Feeding and watering basics ✻ How to become a diaper expert
✻ Sleep tactics ✻ Bodily functions ✻ Washing and dressing basics

"THEY DON'T COME WITH INSTRUCTIONS"

When baby comes home from the hospital, you're going to be surprised by how much everyone forgot to tell you. It's as if the nurses, midwives, doctors—even your own parents—just decided to keep everything a secret so they could take pleasure in watching you fumble with diaper ointments, scramble around trying to sterilize milk bottles, and live on three hours of sleep a night. You might not know the difference between a binkie and a baby's bottle. You might think a rocker is just an old musician with tattoos and long hair. You might be under the dangerous misapprehension that a breast pump is a sex toy. And you might even detect an amused tone in your parents' voices as they claim ignorance to your new plight. "They don't come with instructions," someone might say in lieu of any actual advice. Well, now they do.

It will behoove you to start with some absolute basics. The best advice anyone gave my wife and me after we brought our first son home was that when a baby cries he most likely needs one of three things: food, sleep, or a clean diaper. It's not rocket science—it's more frustrating than that. It's not an exact science at all, which is why you can now prepare yourself for bucketloads of spit-up and lots of burping, plenty of potentially embarrassing songs and dances to get your baby to sleep (even if it's only for 15 minutes, albeit 15 magnificent minutes), and truckloads of stinky diapers.

These important basics represent the key things you need to know. If you don't grasp a whole lot more, you could still make an okay dad. Just don't think it's going to be simple.

FEEDING AND WATERING

A newborn baby's first meal is always either breast milk or a breast milk-like drink called formula that they suck from a bottle. The good thing about having a liquid meal is that baby gets the hydration they need at the same time they're getting the right nutrients. That means there's no need to offer him a glass of water. (Trust me on this one.)

According to the U.S. Department of Health and Human Services and the U.S. Federal Drug Administration (FDA), breastfeeding is the best option for newborn babies. It provides the fats, proteins, and sugars every baby needs (and not just any old fats, proteins, and sugars, but ones that are designed by the mother's body for her baby's specific needs, which vary greatly from baby to baby). Breastfeeding also gives the baby helpful antibodies—the same ones found in Mom's system—to help ward off sickness. Plus, breastfeeding is cheap and always available without needing a sleepy dad to get up in the middle of the night to prepare a bottle.

Now, if you happen to be a single dad with a small infant, then you won't be doing any breastfeeding. Again, just trust me on this one. Also, breastfeeding may not be the best solution for all mothers, some of whom cannot breastfeed for medical reasons and some of whom plan to go back to work soon, making breastfeeding an impracticality. In these cases, infant formula is the best option.

Infant formulas are FDA-approved mixes that provide your baby with similar proteins, fats, and sugars found in breast milk. Nothing can substitute for mother's milk but this stuff comes close. Be prepared to set aside a sizable portion of your paycheck on formula, as most pediatricians recommend feeding it to your young one until his or her first birthday, though by then baby should be tucking into some solids as well.

or her first birthday, though by then baby should be tucking into some solids as well.

Formula comes in powder form (which is the cheapest), liquid concentrate, or ready to eat (which is the most expensive). If you choose the powder or the liquid concentrate, then you're going to need to follow the directions and mix it up. (The recipe will become etched onto your brain after the 500th preparation.) It involves boiling water, so start brushing up on your kitchen skills. And don't think about throwing together a 5-gallon bucket of the stuff and storing it under the sink. Once mixed, formula needs to be refrigerated and consumed within 48 hours.

No matter what type of formula you choose, when it's time to feed baby—which could be as often as eight times a day, depending on how much he or she weighs—you'll need to have some sterilized bottles on hand and make sure the liquid meal is just the perfect warm temperature.

PREPARING A BOTTLE

If you find yourself—gasp!—alone with the baby while Mom is out with the girls making up for lost time, you'll need to know how to feed him. Obviously, you won't need a breast pump. Here's how to get a bottle ready for your young one's kisser.

You will need	STEPS
4 x 5-oz baby bottles with nipples **A way to boil water** **Boiled water** **Infant powdered formula mix**	**1** Make sure the bottle and nipple are sterilized by running them through a hot dishwasher or by buying a bottle sterilizer, which is basically a modified electric vegetable steamer. (Don't be inclined to modify your own.) **2** To make 20 oz of formula—enough for four feeds, depending on weight—boil at least 24 ounces of water for about 5 minutes. You can keep formula in the refrigerator for 48 hours after you've mixed it, and your young bottomless pit—err, baby—will surely have no problem going through this much. (continued on next page)

STEPS (continued)

3 Scoop out enough formula into each 5-oz bottle and add boiling water to each bottle. The instructions on every pack of infant formula will tell you the appropriate ratio of mix to water, and it's very important to get it right. Too little water could upset baby's stomach and too much will dilute the mix so that baby doesn't get the right amount of nutrition. Mix each bottle with a sterilized spoon.

4 If you need to feed baby right away, substantially cool the mixture down first by submerging the bottle in iced water to just under the screw-top nipple. Turn the bottle in the iced water to increase the cooling process. Test the temperature of the formula by putting a few drops of it on the inside of your wrist. It should be body temperature (just like Mom's breast milk), no cooler and certainly no hotter.

5 Heating up a bottle out of the fridge should be done by heating up water on the stove and putting the bottle in the hot water. Never use a microwave, which can heat the formula unevenly and potentially burn your young one's mouth.

TIPS

✓ Don't get caught with a hungry baby and no bottles ready. There are few things more stressful than having to prepare a new batch of formula with a hungry, crying baby in your arms.

✓ It's all the rage for modern moms and dads to use only bottled water for preparing infant formula. If you are concerned about the quality of your tap water, by all means use bottled water. Just remember that bottled water is not always sterilized, so this too needs to be boiled first.

HOW TO KNOW IF BABY IS GETTING ENOUGH MILK

This is definitely something you need to keep an eye on. Newborns should be breastfeeding at least eight times and as often as 12 times a day (roughly every two hours), which means he or she should have between eight and 12 wet or poop-filled diapers a day. Yes, that's right. It's a whole lot of diaper-changing—get used to it. The exception to this may be during the first two or three days after birth, when a baby won't necessarily be hungry after having been hooked up to an all-you-can-eat placenta for nine months. During these times, Mom's breasts are still preparing milk anyway.

Bottle-fed babies may need feeding less frequently because the cows' milk in infant formula doesn't digest as quickly as breast milk, allowing the baby to feel full longer. Generally, bottle-fed babies one to two months old should get 2 to 4 ounces of formula, six to eight times in a 24-hour period. Babies three to five months old should get 6 to 7 ounces of formula five to six times a day. Wet diapers should correspond to the number of feedings.

If your baby isn't having any wet diapers after about the third day of life then you should be concerned and call your doctor. Other signs that baby isn't getting enough milk are dark- or yellow-colored urine (it should be clear or pale) and low weight gain (normal weight gain is roughly 4 to 8 ounces a week). Also, babies who are eating right have really milky, yellow, seedy poop. Get used to it; there should be two or three a day!

SLEEPING PATTERNS

Perhaps the single most excruciating thing about having a newborn, with the exception of unstoppable crying, is the lack of sleep you will be subjected to. But before you curse your bad luck or deliriously try to repay a bad karma debt by flogging yourself publicly, know that most babies don't sleep through the night for very good reasons that have nothing to do with your past youthful diversions.

First of all, babies do sleep quite a bit—the average infant gets about 16 hours a day. The killer is that they don't sleep more than two or three hours at a time for the first few months, and that's what takes its toll on those of us used to recharging for at least seven hours a night. Of course, every baby is different—some might sleep more than 16 hours a day and some less. I've heard of babies who sleep all the way through the night at two months. This was not my baby. He waited until six months to do that, and only then after my wife and I decided it was in everyone's best interests to let him cry it out. Even so, many studies say that the average three-month-old will sleep about eight hours at night and about eight or nine hours during the day. Infants up to three months of age are the ones that require an exceptionally strong constitution of their dads (and, of course, their moms).

The reason babies wake up every few hours is because they need to eat. Even at this early age they have tiny biological alarm clocks inside their tiny bodies that go off like dinner bells throughout the day (and night). There is some discussion about waking your baby to feed him every two or three hours to make sure he's getting enough to eat, but I say this is crazy talk. If your baby is sleeping at night, enjoy it. On the other hand, if you have a reason to suspect that your baby isn't getting enough milk, or if your doctor advises it, then waking a baby during the first six weeks to feed him might be prudent.

Another reason babies might not sleep so soundly for long stretches is because they have shorter sleep cycles than adults, with more REM (rapid eye movement) sleep. That means they're sleeping lighter and dreaming more without getting into that extended deep sleep our bodies long for. Many newborns have restless, jerky sleep, and this is because of the REM. It's nothing to be worried about, as they'll get the hang of deep sleep soon enough. We dads got the hang of deep sleep long ago, but it will be a dim and distant memory for a while.

HOW TO GET YOUR BABY TO SLEEP

Getting your young one down (even if it is for two measly hours) can be tricky, especially because you don't want to botch the job and end up with a tired *and* crying baby—a combination that complicates the task tenfold. No doubt your mother and especially your mother-in-law will offer their advice, which in most cases involves some form of just letting your youngster cry him- or herself to sleep. Following are some more up-to-date tips on how to get your baby some shut-eye.

You will need	STEPS
A quiet, calm environment	1 Look for signs that baby is tired. She might rub her eyes, yawn, or start to get grumpy (which may include crying). If she has just finished eating and her diaper is dry, there's a good chance she wants a nap.
A comfy spot without too many loose fluffy blankets or pillows	2 Rather than just putting baby in her crib or bassinet and leaving the room—a combo that will create a crying baby and some say an emotionally scarred baby with an abandonment complex and a problem with trust—put on some soft music and start to rock baby in your arms. Rocking chairs are great for this.
A sleepy baby	3 Before the baby falls asleep in your arms, just as she's about to drop off, place her in her crib.

(continued on next page)

S T E P S (continued)

4 If it's cold in the house or outside, consider warming up the sheets in baby's bed with a warm towel before putting her down. Cold sheets can be jarring.

5 If she just won't sleep in her crib, try walking her around the block in a stroller that folds down flat. Putting her in a carrier that holds her close to your body and going for a walk also works. Other options are a vibrating chair or self-swinging swing, which can work wonders for sleepy babies.

6 If all else fails, put the baby in her car seat and go for a drive. This works every time.

H I N T

✓ Research done by the American Academy of Pediatrics now shows that it is safer to put babies to sleep on their backs than their stomachs. However, some researchers say that you should put baby on his side, especially if he tends to spit up a lot. Put a rolled-up blanket behind baby so he can't roll onto his back, but don't put baby so far on his side that he'll roll over onto his stomach.

T I P

✓ The risk of letting baby go to sleep in your arms is that she'll start to expect your arms to be there every time she wants to go to bed, which is what's known in child psychology circles as a "crutch." Other crutches include falling asleep while watching TV, falling asleep with a specific stuffed animal, and falling asleep only while breastfeeding. What you want is your baby to learn how to sleep on her own without you or anything else present. That way, when she wakes up in the middle of the night and your arms are asleep with you, the stuffed animal is on the floor, and Mom's breasts are getting their rest, she'll know what to do without needing anything at all.

BODILY FUNCTIONS

If you didn't get a crash course in biology during the birth of your child, then you will certainly get one during the first year of your baby's life. Not only will there be poop—and lots of it—but there will be gas, spit-up, urine, and snot. To keep your knees from buckling under a squeamish stomach, it helps to know why babies emit so many things. It's because their muscles are not yet formed—specifically those muscles we use to hold in urine and feces until we can find a suitable place to put them (which is, most of the time, a toilet). This will happen eventually for your youngster, and then they'll be ready for potty training.

Spitting up is another natural thing that babies do. Usually, baby will lose some of his lunch right after eating, either because he drank too much and he's just getting the level down to the right amount or he's having a good burp and a little milk happens to come along with it. So don't worry, but do plan to wash a lot of shirts. Having "burp clothes" around after baby eats is also a good idea. Keep in mind also that projectile vomiting is not the same thing as spitting up. If your son looses his lunch and it flies across the room, then you should call a doctor.

Also, babies and young children get runny noses a lot, and your instinct is going to be to wipe it as it comes. Be cautious about this, though. Constant nose wiping can lead to red raw noses, which will be painful for baby. You're better off letting the snot come and then giving the nose in question a gentle wipe with a soft, hot rag two or three times a day only.

HOW TO CHANGE BABY

In the first weeks of your baby's life, you will change hundreds of diapers. Soon you'll be able to swap a dry one for a wet one with your eyes closed, which is not such a bad thing—dads have to get their sleep when they can. But before you master the art of the diaper change, you're first going to have to learn to steady a squirming baby and avoid getting peed on while making sure the diaper fits comfortably but snugly.

You will need	STEPS
Changing table or floor	**1** Before you get started, make sure everything you need—diapers, wipes, ointments, and diaper pail—are within easy reach. You don't ever want to leave a baby unattended, so you'll want to keep one hand on him or her at all times. Even the smallest babies have been known to jerk suddenly, and you do *not* want a baby to fall.
Diaper wipes or warm wet cloth	
Diaper rash ointment	**2** Lay baby gently on a changing table, floor, or any other firm surface. Make sure the surface is covered with some kind of washable blanket or pee-proof material.
Cloth or disposable diapers	
Diaper covers with Velcro fasteners (if using cloth diapers)	**3** Take off the diaper by loosening the fasteners on each side.
	4 Lift baby's rear end off the surface by holding his tiny feet in one hand. At the same time, pull the diaper away from his bottom.
	5 If you're dealing with more than just a wet diaper, fold the front of the diaper under baby's bottom so that the poop is covered and you will have a place to rest the dirty bottom while you fish for a diaper wipe. Don't let go of baby's feet or you'll have more than a bottom to clean. Also, if you have a boy, you'd be smart to cover his penis with a cloth while all this is going on or you can count on getting peed on.

(continued on next page)

S T E P S (continued)

6 Gently clean your baby by wiping from front to back with a baby wipe or a soft, warm, wet cloth. This is particularly important for baby girls so that you avoid the possibility of spreading infections. Do a thorough job and be sure to remove all feces.

7 Though our parents may have used talcum powder on our young bottoms, it is frowned upon these days because babies can inhale the dust, which can lead to respiratory problems. Studies have also linked it to ovarian cancer in women. Most pediatricians recommend using a generous amount of diaper ointment instead. It serves as a protective barrier if your baby has diaper rash, and it will keep moisture away from the skin.

8 When you've cleaned up and applied any ointment, hold baby's feet in one hand, lift his bottom off the surface, and slide a fresh diaper under it.

9 Fold the front of the diaper between baby's legs over his front and fasten one side of the diaper and then the other. Make sure the diaper fits snugly around baby's hips and that the tape or Velcro isn't cutting into his skin.

T I P

☑ If you're planning to use cloth diapers, forget pins. They're really only good for sticking sleepy dads in the fingers or crying babies in the gut. Advanced baby technology has given us diaper covers that hold cloth diapers in place like a pair of plastic underwear and fasten across the front with Velcro. They come in small, medium, and large sizes, and can be ordered on the Internet.

H I N T

☑ If baby is getting diaper rash and getting fussy because of it, consider that you're not changing diapers enough. Many pediatricians suggest changing diapers eight to ten times a day—or even double that for cloth diapers!

HOW TO BATHE BABY

Diaper wipes can only clean a baby so much, which is why you'll need to wash her with actual soap and water every few days. In the first weeks, a sponge bath will work fine. Then, as soon as the umbilical cord or a boy's circumcision has completely healed, you can fill up a tiny bath.

You will need	STEPS
Baby bath or large sink **Soft washcloths** **Very mild soap and shampoo** **Soft baby towel with hood**	**1** Whatever you plan to bathe baby in should be filled with warm water. Use the inside of your wrist or forearm to feel the temperature. (Worn, callused, manly hands are often insensitive to water that's too hot.) The water should be only slightly warmer than body temperature. A baby's skin is very sensitive, so take care.
	2 If your house tends to be cold, either from a strong air-conditioner or a weak heater, consider wrapping baby in a towel or blanket before lowering her into the water. Yes, it will get wet and you'll have to dry it, but hey, you're a dad now. Any extra work you do is for the care and protection of your little one.
	3 Gently lower the baby into the water and ALWAYS hold her with one hand and arm, making sure to support her head. Do not leave a small baby alone in even the smallest amount of water. If you've forgotten something, take baby with you (just be sure to wrap her in a dry towel before you do).
	(continued on next page)

S T E P S (continued)

4. Use your other hand and a washcloth to wipe baby's face very gently. Clean her eyes by wiping from near the nose to the outer corners, being careful to catch any little bits of sleep. Wipe behind her ears and in the folds of the ears. It's okay to use cotton swabs on the external parts of a baby's ear, just never put a swab in the ear canal. This can damage the extra-sensitive eardrum.

5. Wash the rest of her body with a washcloth and soap, starting with the neck and working your way down. If it's cold and the baby is wrapped in a towel, uncover one section and then cover it back up as you go.

6. Lastly, use a small amount of shampoo to wash baby's hair (or in many cases, her head). You don't need to lather it up as much as you would your own hair (or head—whatever the case may be). You'll only have to use more water to rinse it off if you do that, which provides more chances for you to get water and soap in baby's face and eyes. Rinse by tilting baby's head back and slowly pouring water over it so that the water runs from front to back, away from her little eyes.

7. Take baby out of the bath, wrap her in a dry towel, and put the hood over her head. Hold her close to let her warm up before putting on a diaper and some clothes.

T I P

 It's always nice to have a bath at night before bedtime. You can feed baby first, give her a bath, and there's a strong chance she'll be out before you finish the first verse of The Wheels on the Bus. Over the years this will become a ritual that your toddler will look forward to.

HOW TO DRESS BABY

When my elder son was an infant I took him to the doctor one June because he had a fever. The first thing the doctor said after having a look at the baby was, "Have you considered the fact that you might be overdressing him?" I looked at her as if to say, "What, you mean he's not suppose to be wearing a sweater over his long-sleeved shirt with pants and wool socks? It can't be more than 85 degrees outside." In other words, babies do tend to be a little colder than we are, but that doesn't mean you have to dress them in sub-zero clothing all the time. As a general rule of thumb, give your baby an extra layer of clothing than what you're wearing.

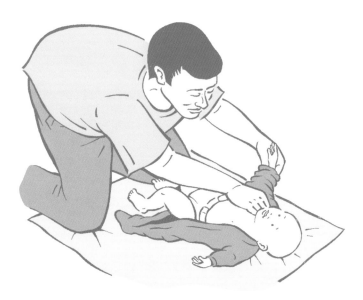

You will need

Loose-fitting, cotton clothing

Pants with snaps in the crotch to make diaper changing easier

Warm knit hats that cover the ears for winter

Mittens in winter

Wide-brimmed hats to keep out summer sun

Pajamas with built-in feet

Socks

DRESSING DO'S AND DON'TS

☑ When pulling on a shirt, be sure to pull open the neck enough so that you can fit baby's head without snagging ears and noses and without having to pull down hard and possibly injuring his neck.

☑ To get arms and legs into clothing, reach into the sleeve or pant leg and gently pull baby's hands and feet through the opening.

☑ Baby socks are notorious for mysteriously coming off. Buy socks for 12-month-olds so that you can pull them high up on a baby's leg and keep them from sliding down.

☑ As tempting as it might be to dress baby to look like a cherub in a fluffy bunny outfit, try to avoid gimmicky baby clothes. On the other hand, having a good laugh at baby's expense might just help lighten the mood.

☑ There are some "clothes" that family and friends give to baby that should be considered optimistic decorative pieces for Christmas day only: white booties, white bonnets and white cardigans are in this category. Useless as hard-wearing, poopable clothing. Leave them in the packet.

TIP

☑ Make getting dressed a fun time by playing peek-a-boo and other silly games. This way, you're less likely to run into resistance.

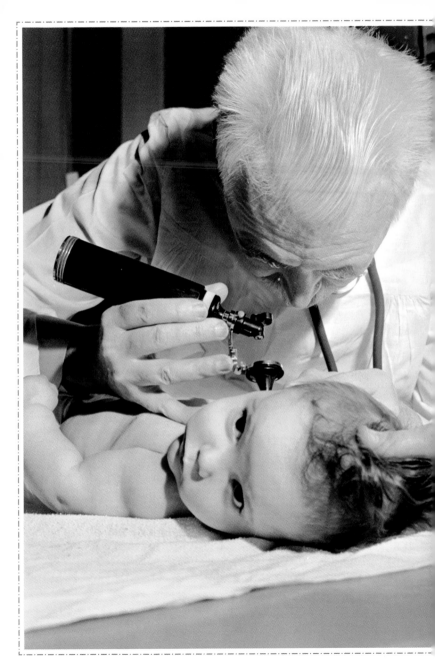

CHAPTER

5

SNIFFS AND COUGHS

AND HOW TO DEAL WITH THEM

In this chapter, you'll learn:

✻ Tell-tale signs of baby's illness: from vomit to diarrhea and other body-fluid malfunctions ✻ What to do at home ✻ When to visit the doctor ✻ Basic first aid

BABY GETS SICK, PARENTS GET CRANKY

You know it's going to happen. You just hope it doesn't happen a lot. Babies get sick, and when they do everyone gets cranky—if not because no one's getting so much sleep then certainly because it's heart wrenching to see your little boy or girl with a fever and an ear infection and not be able to cure it like magic. Plus, all babies and young kids get sick, and that's a good thing because it strengthens their immune systems so that they'll be less likely to get sick as adults. Luckily, there's quite a bit you can do to help your young warrior to get through that which is ailing him.

BABY VOMIT

Spit-up is one thing, but vomit is quite another. While a baby will regularly burp up a smidgen of Mom's milk right after eating, heaving up the entire meal and bathing the whole of your work-day shirt with the contents of her tiny stomach is not a good sign. Chances are she's sick and will need some looking after.

Babies can vomit for a number of reasons, ranging from overeating to indigestion to motion sickness to a stomach virus. In the first few months, a frequent amount of vomiting is to be expected as the baby's digestive system adjusts to the new food. He or she may also be reacting to certain allergens in the breast milk—in those cases moms should consult the doctor and try to screen out foods that might be supplying the allergenic in her breast milk.

After the first few months, increased vomiting may be cause for concern, especially if baby has convulsions, painful or swollen abdomen, vomits over and over for longer than a day, or has traces of blood or stomach bile in the vomit. In these instances, visit your doctor as soon as possible. Lots of vomiting will make baby lethargic and he or she will show signs of dehydration, such as chapped lips, sunken fontanelle ("soft spot" on the baby's head), dry mouth, and infrequent urination.

Projectile vomiting—when the vomit leaves baby's mouth with a force not unlike that of a volcano shooting lava and hot rocks far into the sky—is also cause for alarm.

In the worst cases, such as projectile vomiting or blood or bile in the vomit, consult with your doctor. In most cases, the main thing you want to do at home is keep baby hydrated. Vomiting removes valuable liquids from a body (especially a tiny body), so it's important to replenish them. Dads can do this by first giving baby small amounts of water after baby has stopped puking. If that stays down, go to an electrolyte solution similar to sports drinks—themselves not such a bad option if nothing else is around, though not ideal since they contain lots of sugar, too much of which can deplete the immune system and leave baby vulnerable. Electrolyte solutions are sold at most pharmacies and come in powdered form (to be mixed with water), liquid form, or as a frozen Popsicle. The latter is always a popular option and can help bring down a fever at the same time. Any electrolyte liquid should be given in small quantities and alternated with water every 30 minutes.

If baby hasn't vomited again after about four hours, try feeding a small amount of breast milk or formula. After 24 vomit-free hours, ease back into solid foods with rice cereal or yogurt for a day or two before grilling up a porterhouse steak for the young one. Also, keep up the fluids during this time. Baby should be back to normal spit-ups before you can say, "That's so gross!"

VOMITING DO'S AND DON'TS

☑ Do consult a doctor immediately if baby is projectile vomiting or if there is blood or bile in the vomit.

☒ Don't overreact if your baby spits up a lot. Some say it's a healthy thing since baby is usually burping along with it, relieving herself of gas.

☑ Do check a baby's temperature if she's throwing up.

☑ Do try to keep baby hydrated by giving her a few milliliters of water or electrolyte solution. If baby has trouble keeping that down, try an electrolyte popsicle.

☑ Do ease back into mild solids after a day of water and electrolytes.

☒ Don't hesitate to call your doctor if you think something isn't right.

WHEN THE LEVEE BREAKS

Yes, the bodily fluids keep coming. Dealing with diarrhea can be unpleasant, but consider that baby wears a diaper, which will prevent the poo from getting all over everything like vomit does. (Or at least that's the idea; there's no doubt that diarrhea has been known to squirt out the side of a diaper or two onto Dad's perfectly placed hands or all over his nice new linen pants.)

And just because your three-month-old has frequent watery poops doesn't mean he has the runs. Breastfed babies are supposed to have runny stools. It's after three months that you should be concerned. That's when baby should have one or two dirty diapers a day and they should be a bit more firm.

If you see mucous in the stool—a truly disgusting situation that looks like snot mixed with shit—then that is always cause for concern. When solid foods are introduced and you get frequent runny stools, you can be certain that's diarrhea. Also, if baby's poo suddenly changes from "just a bit squishy" to "runny as hell," that's the trigger for you to spring into action. Babies can get a bout of diarrhea for a number of reasons: from a gastrointestinal (stomach flu) infection, a reaction to a course of antibiotics, food poisoning or a food allergy, through to an enzyme deficiency.

No matter when your young one has a case of the runs, he probably doesn't feel so great, so don't get too angry when you discover that baby's excrement has seeped through his diaper and his pants onto the carpet. Luckily, there are a few things you can do to help baby get through this most unpleasant phase.

WHAT TO DO IF BABY HAS DIARRHEA

☑ Young babies can get diarrhea as part of just about any sickness, from the common cold to teething, so help keep baby healthy by staying healthy yourself.

☑ Prevent diarrhea by making sure your hands are washed frequently and thoroughly—especially after changing a poopy diaper. The micro-organism that causes gastrointestinal infections and diarrhea enters the intestinal tract through the mouth, which essentially means you or your baby has to eat something pretty dirty to get it.

☑ If and when your baby does get diarrhea, it's important to keep him hydrated with electrolytes if he's old enough to be able to take them in. It's more important with diarrhea than with vomiting not to give baby drinks with high sugar, fructose (fruit sugar), or corn syrup contents. Sugar creates more fluid in the intestines and could make the diarrhea worse, and too much fruit juice will also loosen things up down there.

☑ Keep on feeding baby solid foods, if he's eating them already. If baby is on breast milk or formula, stick with that.

☑ Over-the-counter diarrhea medicine should be given only after talking to your doctor.

☑ Change diapers frequently and try to be extra gentle. Diarrhea can bring on painful diaper rash, which is a whole other can of worms. Most bottom creams will prevent irritation, so go ahead and slather some on before it's too late.

☑ While the various nuances of baby's diarrhea may be fascinating to you, don't burden our friends and relatives with details.

ALL PLUGGED UP

Perhaps the one thing worse than diarrhea for baby's digestive system is constipation. This happens when baby isn't getting enough liquids. Rather than constant poop there's no poop, or at least none that comes out; it's stuck in the digestive tract and can be very painful. Constipation is very rare in breastfed babies and unusual in bottle-fed babies. It's when you start getting into the solids that the system can get all backed up.

You can tell if your baby is constipated if he has a hard abdomen and if gets red in the face and grunts a lot but gets no joy and poops only a small dark pellet that may or may not be streaked with blood (lack of fluids and hard stools can cause the lining of the rectum to crack and bleed when the stool is passed). This can be painful for little bodies, which is why they'll love you even more if you can help them out.

WHAT TO DO IF BABY HAS CONSTIPATION

- ☑ If your baby is breastfeeding or bottle-feeding and still has constipation, your best bet is to make an appointment at the doctor. He or she can prescribe medicine to get things moving again.

- ☑ If baby is on solids, purée some prunes, get some prune juice, or chop up some dried prunes into very small bits and feed them to him.

- ☑ Many other fruits, save bananas, can be great clog-busters because of their high fiber content, as can many vegetables. Try blending fruit smoothies with a little bran added.

- ☑ Cut back on constipating foods such as bananas, rice cereal, and cheese.

- ☑ To relieve abdominal pain and gas, bicycle baby's legs or gently push his knees up to his stomach a few times.

THE COMMON COLD

There's nothing sadder than a baby with a cold. Snot runs unabated. Little coughs and sneezes wake you up at night. Eyes get blurry and red. It's all caused by a virus that has been passed on to baby from dirty hands or someone else who has coughed or sneezed in her direction. The best way to prevent a cold is to keep your and any older kids' hands washed, and to ask anyone to wash their hands before holding baby. Also, keep baby away from people who do have colds. They'll understand. If they don't, tough.

WHAT TO DO IF BABY HAS A COLD

☑ Give older babies lots of fluids and vitamin C. Babies who are breastfeeding have all the fluids they need. They're less likely to get a cold anyway because they have their mom's immunities during that time.

☑ Put on a vaporizer while baby is sleeping to help open up nasal passageways.

☑ Elevate baby's head while she is sleeping by propping the mattress up with a rolled-up towel.

☑ Babies less than one year old should only get cold medicine like decongestants if you've okayed it with the doctor.

☑ Water is the best decongestant on the market. Your child might even like it for a change.

☑ Give older babies pineapple. The enzymes in it help break down thick mucus and help with decongestion.

☑ For earaches due to nasal congestion, fill up a sock with cornmeal and heat it until it's warm to the touch. Then use it as a heating pad against baby's ear. Works every time.

A FEVERISH BABY

Lots of things can give a small baby a fever: teething, a cold, allergies, new immunizations, or too many blankets, to name a few. And most of the time, a fever is a good thing; it's how the body fends off invading bacteria and viruses. As a general rule, babies tend to have higher fevers than adults do, so unless the temperature is over 100°F, then there's really no reason for concern, especially if baby is eating normally. It's when baby's fever approaches 102°F or higher that you should freak out. Just kidding. Freaking out never helps. Take note of baby's behavior. If she is lethargic, has stopped eating, or is crying a lot, then you should call your doctor. In the meantime, calmly try a few of the following steps.

WHAT TO DO IF BABY HAS A FEVER

- ✓ If baby is bundled up, try removing the blankets and the sweaters. Many times, that will drop the temperature at least a little.

- ✓ Give the appropriate dose of infant's acetaminophen (brand name: Tylenol) or ibuprofen. For the youngest babies, check to make sure this is okay with your doctor.

- ✓ Get a cloth wet with warm water, wring it out, and gently smooth the damp cloth over baby's forehead, neck, and body, letting the water air-dry on her skin. Take care not to use cold water and definitely do not put baby in a tub of cold water. That can actually have the reverse effect and raise the temperature, as the body has to work harder to overcome the shock of having cold water put on it.

- ✓ Turn down heaters and turn on a fan.

- ✓ Keep baby hydrated either with breast milk or, if she's eating solids, water or a water-electrolyte solution.

HOW TO CHECK TEMPERATURE

Knowing how high (or low) a temperature is usually isn't the first indication that your baby is sick. First you will have noticed a change in his mood—he's become cranky, restless, or low in energy, or he's pukign up a storm. Second, you probably have an idea that he has a fever simply by touching his forehead with your lips—a time-tested method for temperature-taking by moms and dads the world over. Taking temperature with a thermometer can reinforce what you already know ("Yup, he has a temperature all right") and it can be a way to see if medicine or other treatments are working or not.

Having a good thermometer around the house is essential, and there are several different kinds: the ear thermometer, the underarm thermometer, and yes, the anal thermometer. Oral thermometers just don't work with infants or even toddlers, not because they don't have a temperature under their tongues but because it's impossible to get even the slimmest cooperation from your crying, squirming young one. In fact, you should know that taking a baby's temperature with any thermometer would be the easiest thing in the world if not for his constant protests. Dealing with that is the hard part. Any time you take a baby's temperature, no matter what the method, make sure he is as calm as you can possibly make him (easier said than done, I know). Intense crying can raise the body temperature and give you a distorted reading.

Finally, don't persist beyond reasonable attempts. If baby is very uncomfortable and struggling actively and mightily, then remove the thermometer and try a different method a little later on.

EAR OR TYMPANIC THERMOMETER

For basic ease of use these are the best kind to get—though some doctors warn that it can be difficult to place the thermometer in the ear canal exactly right, especially in small babies younger than three months. In some cases doctors will even ask you to double-check the temperature using a different method, which kind of makes what you just did a waste of time. In theory, what you do is simply put the end of the thermometer in baby's ear, press a button and in seconds you have an accurate temperature. The idea is that there's very little struggling to get the job done and it offers the least discomfort for baby. In addition to some doctors' concerns, another drawback to these is they cost far more than the other kinds. The best thing to do if you get one of these is to ask the doctor to show you how to use it properly.

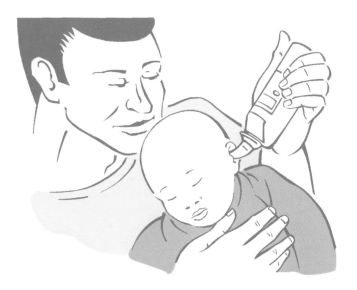

RECTAL THERMOMETER

This is the most accurate method for taking a baby's temperature as it measures heat at the body's core. Temperatures taken anally will be a full degree higher than those taken orally. So, if 98.6°F is the normal body temperature taken orally, 99.6°F is the norm anally.

You will need	STEPS
Rectal thermometer	1 Wash the thermometer with cold water and soap.
Petroleum jelly	2 Rub petroleum jelly on about an inch of the bulb-end of the thermometer.
Tissue paper	3 Place baby on his belly on your lap, with a blanket or pillow under his hips.
	4 With one hand, spread the buttocks and with the other place about an inch of the bulb end of the thermometer gently into the anus.
	5 Hold the thermometer in place between your middle and ring fingers while placing the palm of your hand over the baby's bottom. Use your other hand to help hold baby's head up. Do this for two minutes.
	6 After two minutes, take the thermometer out, wipe clean with tissue paper and read it.

DO'S AND DON'TS

✓ Do constantly soothe baby while you're taking his temperature by talking to him or singing lullabies.

✗ Don't force the thermometer.

UNDERARM OR AUXILLARY THERMOMETER

The most common thermometer and the easiest to use—especially for squirmy babies—is the kind that you put under baby's armpit. Most baby supply stores sell these with digital readouts that are run on small camera batteries. They're reliable, cheap, and you shouldn't ever have to change the battery, even if Dad forgets to push the "off" button after use—they'll automatically turn off to save juice. Oral thermometers or rectal ones will work if placed snuggly in a baby's armpit; it just takes about five minutes to get a reading and really it's not worth it. Temperatures taken under the arm are a full degree lower than what is normal orally, so always add a degree to an underarm temperature.

You will need	STEPS
Underarm thermometer	1. Remove baby's shirt and sit him in your lap. Make sure his underarm is dry.
	2. Lift up baby's arm and place the end of the thermometer in his armpit so that the thermometer rests in the fold of his arm.
	3. Lower baby's arm over the thermometer and hold his elbow against his side with one hand. Make sure the thermometer is in fact snug under the arm and not sticking out the other side.
	4. With your other hand, stroke baby's head or give a finger puppet show as a distraction.
	5. Digital underarm thermometers blink off and on until an accurate temperature has been taken. This can take about three minutes.

TEETHING

Teething is what happens when a baby's first teeth begin pushing through the gums into full-fledged chompers. This usually happens around six months, though it can be as early as three months and as late as one year. In most cases, you'll be able to see the end of the tooth on the gum, starting with the bottom incisors first, then the top front ones (the last molars will come in around age three).

If you don't see a tooth, you can guess a baby is teething if he's drooling a lot, has a low fever or diarrhea, and is eager to chew on things. As you can imagine, it's a painful time and many babies get irritable. You can't stop the teeth from coming in, so the best you can do is make baby as comfortable as possible.

HOW TO HELP A TEETHING BABY

☑ Teething babies like to chew on things—anything—because the pressure on the gums and new teeth coming in helps relieve the pain. Teething rings, teething biscuits, or even fingers will help.

☑ Cold things to chew on feel good for baby and it helps numb the pain a little. Try giving her a frozen banana; a clean, icy washcloth; or a cold carrot stick.

☑ Chill a teething ring in the freezer before giving it to her.

☑ Rub your fingers gently on her gums—be sure to give your hands a good wash first. It might hurt her a bit at first but she'll soon find that the pressure feels good.

☑ If baby is eating solids, cold applesauce and yogurt are welcome foods.

☑ An infant dose of acetaminophen will help the pain and reduce fever if she has one. Check with your doctor before doing this.

THINGS THAT GO BUMP IN THE NIGHT–AND DAY

Babies are prone to all kinds of cuts, bumps, scrapes, bug bites, and other minor injuries. But this is nothing compared with when they start crawling and certainly before they start wobbling around on two feet. You might like to show off your childhood scars in the bar with your pals, but baby won't be so delighted to show you her bumps and bruises and she'll darn well let you know when she's hurt herself on the edge of the coffee table.

Minor injuries are a part of life as baby begins to explore her world (albeit it in an often haphazard way). But she needs you to look out for her with more than just a soothing word and a cuddle. Now is not the time to tell baby to buck up and to take it on the chin 'cause the world ain't a friendly place. Now is the time to accept baby is prone to scrapes, to protect her as much as you can without stifling her space to explore, and to brush up on your strapping dad-to-the-rescue routine. Think of it as a chance for your little one to begin looking up to you in awe and wonder as their hero. You know it won't last long.

Following are some words of advice for how to treat more common, minor ailments.

CUTS AND SCRAPES

Sometimes it's baffling how they happen. The fact is they do. Cuts and scrapes are a fact of life, especially for older babies who are crawling, pulling up, and just learning to walk. If you're baby gets a bump, here's what to do.

You will need	**STEPS**
Warm water and soap	1. If a cut or scrape is bleeding, apply direct pressure until the bleeding stops.
Washcloth	2. For cuts, wash the area with warm water and soap to remove any dirt. If dirt is present in the cut, try to get it out by running warm water over the cut to flush it out. Don't poke around in the cut to get dirt out, which may cause more damage.
Cotton balls	
Band-aids	
	3. Scrapes need washing too. Use a washcloth or a cotton ball soaked with warm water, and gently dab the scrap or abrasion to remove any dirt.
	4. Cover the cut or scrape with a Band-aid.
	5. If the cut or scrape is minor, uncover the area at night to let the wound dry out and heal faster. Cover again in the morning if need be. If you notice any signs of infection, such as redness, swelling, and pus, take baby to the doctor.

BURNS

From hot coffee or tea to a long day at the beach, babies have the chance of burning themselves more often than we'd like to think. There are some who say that once they burn themselves they won't do it again, but that sounds shaky to me (and perhaps even criminal). Does that mean we shouldn't put a screen in front of the fireplace or we should leave the broiler door open with baby in the room? Not a chance. A better option is to get baby to pre-school age and beyond without ever burning themselves. At that point you can reason with them and tell them it will hurt. Simply put, avoid burns at all costs.

When you are cooking (yes, we dads do literally put food on the table at times), drinking hot coffee, barbecuing, ironing (okay, this might be a stretch), or doing anything else that involves flame or heat, keep a watchful eye on baby. If she gets too close to something, a quick, loud "hey" or "no" will definitely get her attention. She might start crying because you startled her, but it's better than a burn that smarts for the rest of the evening.

In fact, the sooner baby learns to heed your words and pick up on the attitude with which you say them, the better. You only have one pair of hands, and sometimes you won't be able to catch baby as quickly as she might pull at a cord or touch a heater. We men aren't always the best at multitasking, but becoming a dad is a quick way to develop the skill of having eyes in the back of your head. The goal here is to foster a relationship with baby in which they know that Dad is looking out for them. Baby should know that obeying Dad's instructions and heeding his verbal warnings are really good ideas.

You will need	STEPS
Cold water	1. Fill up a sink with cool tap water and soak burned fingers hands or feet until baby calms down and the pain seems to go away.
Wash rags	2. If soaking is impractical, use cold compresses (a cool wash cloth soaked with tap water will work fine) until the pain subsides.
Moisturizing cream	3. For sunburns, use cold compresses for about 10 minutes at a time, roughly three times a day or any time baby seems troubled by the burn.
Calamine lotion	4. After applying the compresses, apply moisturizing cream or calamine lotion.
Band-aids	5. In both cases, consider giving baby acetaminophen or some other pain reliever to make her more comfortable. It's always good to consult your doctor before doing this.

DO'S AND DON'TS

☑ Do prevent sunburns by keeping babies fully covered in lightweight clothing and sun hats.

☒ Don't put ice directly on any kind of burn as it can damage the skin (frostbite) and make things worse.

☒ Don't use petroleum jelly on a sunburn because it clogs pores, seals out air, and does not help the healing process.

THE DANGER OF FINGERNAILS

Sorry guys, we are not talking about scratches on your back from wild nights of sex with your woman, we are talking about baby. Tiny fingernails seem to grow faster than you can down a beer. What this means is that there's a really good chance that your baby will scratch her face as she tries to put her hands in her mouth (and starting at two months, she will try this). This not only makes her look like she just got into a fight with the family cat, but it makes Mom and Dad look bad too, as if you weren't paying attention while the cat danced on your child's head.

To avoid a visit from your neighborhood social worker, be sure to keep baby's fingernails trimmed. The best tool for this is fingernail scissors as opposed to the clippers, which aren't as safe and are harder to use. Babies don't like this much, so the best times to trim their nails are when they're sleepy or breastfeeding.

In the latter case you'll probably get away with just handing Mom the fingernail scissors. If the task is left to you, hold baby's hand firmly with one hand while you trim with the other. They'll try to pull away but will be no match for your superior strength. Once you get the nails sufficiently trimmed, smooth out the sharp edges with an emery board. Since baby fingernails grow surprisingly fast, be prepared to get out the scissors a couple of times a week.

If you just can't get around to it that often, you can buy baby clothes made with built-in hand covers on the sleeves. Just pull them right over baby's hands at night. It may look like the little one is wearing a straightjacket, but at least she won't scratch herself.

BABY INJURY PRECAUTIONS

☑ Never shake a baby. It sounds like commonsense, but rates of "shaken baby syndrome" are on the increase. Little baby's skull and brain is much more delicate than yours and if shaken vigorously, your baby can sustain massive injuries. If your baby is crying continually and you're way beyond the end of your tether, don't be too proud to ask for help from a family member and/or pediatrician. It's also a good idea, if you have a fussy baby, to warn other caregivers of the dangers of shaking baby.

☑ When changing a baby, keep one hand on her at all times. Consider getting a changing table with sides that might also prevent baby from rolling off onto the floor.

☑ Don't put baby down on a couch or chair alone—she can roll off or roll into pillows that might cover her face.

☑ SIDS (Sudden Infant Death Syndrome) is the leading cause of death in babies between one month and four months of age and doctors still can't explain it. What scientists do know is that soft bedding holds serious risks for little noses and windpipes. Don't be tempted to load up your baby's crib with the fluffy stuff. Check with your doctor also for the latest wisdom on positioning your baby when you put her to bed. And you can watch for warning signs such as a tendency towards sleep apnea—episodes in which baby stops breathing for several seconds during sleep. Treating apnea may involve clearing obstructed air passageways or treating an infection, both of which can be done at a hospital.

☑ Past histories of SIDS in the family should be a warning sign as well. There is also evidence that there is an increased risk of SIDS in children whose mothers have smoked during the pregnancy. If you're concerned about SIDS, talk to your doctor.

THE CRYING GAME

In this chapter, you'll learn:

* The top ten reasons why babies cry
* How to interpret a whimper, a cry, and a wail
* Techniques to get baby to stop screeching
* How to cope with the dreaded colic

WHAT DOES IT MEAN?

You'd think that with all the advances in medical and genetic technology, someone would have figured out a way for babies to be born with the power of speech. They wouldn't have to talk politics or anything; they would only have to tell us what they want. "Dad, this diaper is feeling a bit stale. Can you help me out here?" is a far more agreeable way to communicate than getting red in the face and crying until snot runs out your nose and you throw up. But alas, they cannot. Babies cry and that's that.

Until your baby is pointing or managing a few audible grunts that only you can translate, chances are you're going to be guessing exactly what it is that baby wants when she's crying.

For new dads this means many, many agonizing, frustrating, and maddening late nights. Know now that a baby's cry has to be one of the most stressful sounds in all of life—something equivalent would be a helicopter making a surprise landing in your living room. So stressful, in fact, that you will experience a confusing emotional mixture of wanting to fight off the evils torturing the infant (if only you could find them) and wanting to throw the inconsolable bundle out the window.

To avoid the latter option, it helps to know that babies cry for a reason. First of all, a crying baby doesn't mean you're a bad dad or that someone switched your baby with an alien devil child when you weren't looking. Infants that cry are normal and healthy. If they aren't crying, then you really have something to worry about.

HOW TO TELL
WHAT BABY WANTS

It's always advisable to ask yourself about the three basics: Does baby need a new diaper? Is she hungry? Is she tired? A wet diaper will be easy enough to detect. A good indicator that baby is hungry is if she starts to root around on your chest with her mouth, looking for the milk-filled boob you do not have. Tired babies, on the other hand, will have red eyes that even the youngest ones will rub with their tiny fists. They'll also do a fair bit of yawning between cries. A few other things to check include diaper rash, which you can ease with a cream; temperature, which can be lowered with infant medicine; and gas, which can be loosed with a few gentle pats on the back.

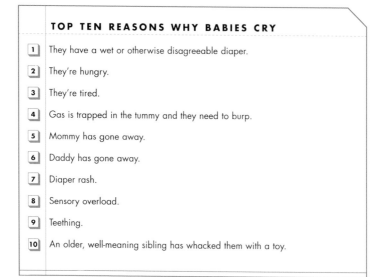

TOP TEN REASONS WHY BABIES CRY

1. They have a wet or otherwise disagreeable diaper.
2. They're hungry.
3. They're tired.
4. Gas is trapped in the tummy and they need to burp.
5. Mommy has gone away.
6. Daddy has gone away.
7. Diaper rash.
8. Sensory overload.
9. Teething.
10. An older, well-meaning sibling has whacked them with a toy.

HOW TO COPE WITH A CRYING BABY

1. Know that the crying will eventually stop.

2. Know that most of the time there is something you can do to help (see opposite).

3. Take pleasure in the fact that you are caring for baby in his hardest moments. Yes, he is aware that you're there holding him.

4. Put baby down for a minute and leave the room for a deep breath and a relaxing drink of water before going back in. Leaving baby alone to cry for a few minutes won't scar him for life.

5. Ask someone else to sit with baby for a while, even if it's a neighbor or friend, so you can gather your strength.

6. Bring forward that urgent business trip to Rio.

HOW TO STOP THE CRYING

When a small baby cries it means they really are trying to tell you something, and it's usually something quite simple. Poop, food, sleep. Poop, food, sleep. Get the picture? This is the life of your small baby and this is the mental checklist you'll have down rote before the end of your first few hours looking after them. Your parents and every adult in your (now diminishing) social circle will likely give you advice on getting baby to stop crying. And they will tell it to you in the most confident of manners. Of course, the answer is to do what works for baby and you—but did I mention "poop, food, sleep"?

Following are the tried-and-true techniques employed by tired but successful dads the world over:

	TOP WAYS TO GET YOUR BABY TO STOP CRYING
1	Check the diaper. No one likes to wear soggy or poo-filled underwear.
2	Try feeding the little rascal.
3	It might be that your youngster is tired and needs help getting to sleep. This leads to suggestions 4 through 8, the sleeping-baby canon (read on).
4	Offer a pacifier or your washed pinkie finger for baby to suck on.
5	Swaddle small babies so they'll feel secure and/or hold baby against the warmth of your tummy.
6	Take a stroll with baby in the baby carrier, or rock gently in a rocking chair.
7	Take baby for a drive. Around and around the block we go.
8	Sing softly or play an instrument for him (depending on your musical ability and assuming the trumpet isn't your instrument of choice).

THE MADNESS OF COLIC

If you find that your baby is crying (and verging on screaming) for hours every afternoon, it could be that he or she has colic. This phenomenon, which doctors still don't know the exact cause of, usually starts in infants around the second week and can continue through the sixth month. Intense gas pain, hormonal withdrawal from Mom's system, and over-stimulation from this brand-new world are all theories used to explain colic. For dads like you and me, though, all we care about is how to comfort the baby and find a way to deal with the crying.

There is a medicine that some doctors prescribe for colicky babies. It comes in several brand names but the active ingredient is simethicone, an anti-gas medicine. But this medicine doesn't always work, and it has been known to make matters worse. A better approach is to try to calm your baby—and the place to start is for you to stay calm yourself. This is, of course, easier said than done, but if baby senses that you or Mom is tense, they may have a hard time relaxing. Following are some more ways to help with colic.

THINGS NOT TO DO WITH A CRYING BABY

- [X] Head down to the local library and try to write your Ph.D. thesis.
- [X] Take her to a board meeting.
- [X] Take a long-haul flight with three stopovers.
- [X] Get on crowded public transportation at rush hour.
- [X] Leave her in the car (even though you might feel like it).
- [X] Try to reason with her.

SOMETIMES BABY JUST CRIES

Sometimes when a baby cries nothing works. They might have no particular problem you can detect, and no matter how many times you drive around the block or how much the baby eats or has attention from friendly faces, the poor little guy or girl will cry and cry and cry. So once you've checked all the basics (diaper, food, sleep), and after you've done all you can to comfort your child, it's time to rethink—or rather, unthink—your approach.

Instead of trying to solve the problem, which is any dad's natural response, realize that there is no problem. All babies cry. You cried when you were this age and you turned out okay (well, mostly). The trick is to get used to the crying as much as you possibly can. Now all you can do is hold your boy or girl close and simply let them be a baby.

And it does help to hold baby rather than leave them in their crib for long periods of time to cry it out—doing this will only leave baby feeling helpless and the crying will last longer. Try carrying baby around with you in a sling, so that they know they're not alone, and attempt to get on with some of the tasks in life other than soothing a crying baby. You won't be able to write your thesis or have long, meaningful conversations with family and friends during these times, but you might just bring yourself to get some vacuuming done or take a walk in the local park. Sometimes the movement and change of atmosphere will benefit both of you.

Then when you can't stand it anymore, wake up your wife, girlfriend, or whoever else happens to be in the house with you, hand the baby over and let them rethink—or unthink—things for a while.

PLAYTIME!

(FOR YOU AND BABY)

In this chapter, you'll learn:

✻ If you're a Dad or a Dud ✻ "Tuba in the Belly" and "This Little Piggy"
✻ How to swim with baby ✻ How to teach a new baby old tricks

THE IMPORTANCE OF PLAY

Play is often cited by experts as being the key to learning at a very early age. Indeed, a child's brain grows faster in his first two years of life than at any other time, and by playing kids explore, make sense of, and learn about the world around them and how they fit into that world both physically and emotionally. So in a sense, the more play you encourage, the smarter your child is becoming and the faster he or she will adjust to their surroundings. (Note: Watching cartoons on television is not playing.)

Play is also a great way for dads to create a bond with and get close to their offspring, especially if Dad happens to feel left out or distant from their cute but oblivious bundle of joy. And believe me, if you feel this way, you're not alone. Anyway, who wants to change diapers, wipe away spit-up, and help baby get to sleep all the time? Besides, too much work all the time turns Dad into a dud.

HOW PLAY HELPS BONDING

For those who are having trouble getting involved in their baby's early life, playing will bring you closer because the physical touch and eye contact that comes with playing helps babies feel safe and loved while helping Dad feel connected. We're not talking about doing science experiments or building doll houses here—that will come later. Play with a three-month-old can be as easy as smiling, talking, and staring into her eyes. Simple games like peek-a-boo from behind a blanket will delight a six-month-old for hours. Just going for a walk with baby in a carrier or holding a baby so he can sit or stand on your chest is beneficial for everyone. Playing is different than just attending to your baby's needs. It's physical, active, lighthearted, and often silly—four things dads know plenty about.

For baby, playing can give her an early sense of self-esteem that can last into the adult years. When you show that you're interested and want to spend time with her, she feels important. Play also encourages confidence and independence. If one day she wants to pick up the rattle herself without you handing it to her, let her. The earlier she can get that "I did it!" response, the less she'll have to deal with issues of self-worth later on.

For dads, play allows you to get to know your baby, which means you're getting involved in her life right from the start. Do you have a laid-back child or one who has a sparkle of high energy in her eye? Does baby like a little roughhousing or does she prefer gentle rocking instead? Whatever the case, you'll never know unless you get down on the floor and play with your kids. That also means they'll get to know you too.

WHAT'S IN A GAME?

Play is not just a way to kill time until dinner. Far from it. Play is how children build muscle, gain strength, and learn coordination. It's also how they explore the great big scary and exciting world around them. The more they play, the more they understand how the world works, how their emotions work, and how they can succeed on the playgrounds of childhood and, later, of life. The games you play should encourage independence, confidence, and self-esteem.

Games for baby and Daddy time

GAME	HOW IT WORKS
Peek-a-Boo	This old standard works wonders, as it probably has since the dawn of time. Just put your face behind a towel, blanket, or your hand, pop your face out and say the magic words. It gets a smile every time.
Tuba in the Belly	Place your mouth on baby's belly and blow until you make a rasping tuba-like sound and baby shrieks with joy.
This Little Piggy	Pulling tiny toes helps baby get to know his body, and listening to Dad say a story rhyme helps baby giggle.
Pitch and Catch	Wait until baby gets older before you start throwing her in the air and catching her. If she cries or seems to be scared, stop immediately. You can test the water by zooming her around without letting go. Don't do this around Mom and definitely don't drop baby.
Who's That?	Hold baby in front of a mirror and say, "Who's that?" Point to nose, ears, chins, and eyes to help baby get to know the names of things and to hear your voice.
Name Game	Walk around the room with baby in a front carrier and point to and name everything in his room. Babies love to hear your voice, and the more you and your partner talk to them the faster they'll pick up talking.
Reading	Get a soft book or board book—something baby can chew on while you show her the pictures and read the words.
Bath Time	Take a bath with baby.
Walking Game	Even at the youngest ages, babies will instinctively move one foot in front of the other while you hold them up.

GOOD GAMES TO PLAY
WITH BABY IN GROUPS

Babies don't play with other children until well into their toddler years, but you will often have friends and family come over to see baby and to marvel at your new domestic lifestyle. And that's a good thing. It helps you stay connected, and it generates a type of second family and support group for your baby—which gives baby a wider range of experiences with which to make sense of their world. So when friends or family stop by, one great way to involve them with baby is to play games.

Games for the group

GAME	HOW IT WORKS
Reading	Take turns reading one story with a family member or friend. Maybe you each can be different characters. Baby might not understand your words but he'll love hearing those different voices.
Sheet Swing	Put baby in the middle of a sheet while you and a friend securely hold the sides. Then gently swing her back and forth.
Walking Game	For babies, just learning to pull up and stagger around is new and exciting. You can sit in a circle on the ground with friends or family and help baby go from one person to the next.
Bath Time	Friends and family will be flattered to help with baby's bath time. You might even manage to get them to do the whole thing.

NEW BABY OLD TRICKS

If you exhaust all the games, massages, and exercises, you'll be happy to know there's more, lots more. Plus it's always a good thing to head out into new territory.

One great thing dads can do with their babies is set them up in front of the loudspeakers and play music for them. Don't worry about baby becoming a doped-up rock star. You'll have plenty of time for that type of thing in about 12 years. Research has shown that infants who listen to music gain weight faster, have lower blood pressure, and stronger heartbeats than infants who don't. I'm willing to bet that the research wasn't done while those babies were listening to gangsta rap or death metal, so find something nice and soothing. Make sure it's something you like too so you can entertain baby with your dancing and singing.

A good active alternative you can do with baby is to go swimming. Just make sure you're not tagging along with the local Polar Bear Swimming chapter. The water needs to be warm. A bathtub is a great place to help baby swim. Just hold onto his tummy and gently move him back and forth in the tub, making extra specially sure to keep his mouth and chin above water. Also, it never hurts to throw in good sound effects and pretend he's a powerboat or spaceship or something.

If you haven't figured it out already, the key to having fun with small babies is keeping it simple. Hold a brightly colored ball in front of a three-month-old's eyes and move it from side to side. She'll no doubt follow it with her eyes.

Also, any time you're holding baby, simply talking to her about the world is as much fun as she can imagine right now. Holding her up to a flower and saying, "Flowers smell good" is great. Or try, "This is Daddy's new car. Daddy financed this car and got a really good interest rate." She'll smile as if you were feeding her chocolate.

BABY MASSAGE

Okay, so babies don't do much working out or heavy lifting, and they don't get sore the way we do after sitting at the office all day in a poorly made desk chair. But with all this game playing they do use those muscles. Besides, baby massage isn't all about working the pain out of tight muscles—and no, you shouldn't expect baby to reciprocate with a shoulder rub for you. Massaging your young one is a great way for the two of you to bond. It's relaxing, it stimulates baby muscles, and some say gently massaging the stomach can help ease gas pains in the stomach. Massaging your baby may even help improve sleep patterns and strengthen her tiny immune system. Regardless, it's a good fun, physical thing you and baby can do to spend time together. Babies love to be touched.

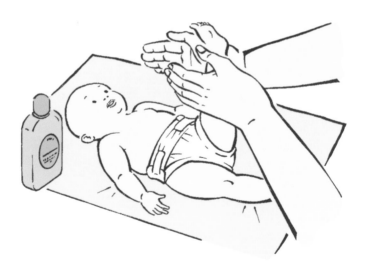

You will need	STEPS
Baby lotion or baby oil **A quiet, warm room** **A towel** **About 15 minutes**	**1** Touching mainly with the palms of both hands, gently spread your hands over baby's head. Repeat three times. **2** Use the palms of your hands to rub baby's chest by placing your hands together in a prayer manner. With hands together and your thumbs closest to you, gently touch the center of baby's chest with your pinkies. Now slowly open your hands outward over baby's chest so that your fingers and palms touch him soothingly. **3** Repeat step 2 on baby's back. **4** Massage baby's arms by "milking" them. Very gently grip baby's arm with one hand and pull it towards baby's wrist as if you were milking a cow. When one hand gets to the wrist, start with the other hand just under the shoulder and so on. **5** Repeat step 4 on baby's legs. **6** Next, roll baby's arms gently between your hands. Place the arm on one palm and sandwich it with the other hand. Rapidly "roll" baby's arm back and forth in a quick, short manner. **7** Repeat step 6 on baby's legs.

TIP

✓ Baby massage is not like adult massage, so don't start Rolfing baby with the deep-tissue techniques your karate teacher showed you. Be gentle—gentler than you think—and stop if baby seems uncomfortable.

EXERCISING BABY

Like play, exercising your baby is a good way to spend time with her while promoting good coordination and muscle development. There's no need to go out and buy a mini treadmill or a tiny stationary bike. This is a lot simpler and a lot cheaper. And while strapping baby into a jogging stroller while you exercise is recommended, that's not what we're after here either. Helping your baby move her arms and legs and use her muscles isn't about "no pain no gain." It's about relaxing with your infant, bonding, and having fun. A 10-minute session a day is all it takes, and you can do it while changing her diaper.

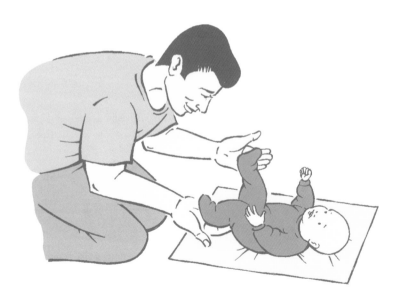

EXERCISES DAD CAN DO FOR BABY

1. The smallest babies will instinctively hold onto your finger when you place it in their hands. This can help strengthen arm and hand muscles. It's also damn cute.

2. When baby is around two or three months, lay her on her stomach so she can strengthen her neck muscles as she tries to look up. Some babies love this; some babies hate it. You'll soon find out which your baby is.

3. At about three months old, baby will begin to show signs of being able to grip things. Help her out by handing her a rattle. When she drops it, hand it to her again. Rubber and plastic rings work well for this too.

4. Also at about three or four months, baby will have good control over neck muscles and should be able to hold her head up. (If not then skip this exercise.) You can promote stomach strength by holding baby's hands and pulling her up to a sitting position. Once she has this one down, you can pull her all the way up to a stand.

5. Bicycle baby's legs back and forth by placing her on her back, holding her feet, and gently moving her legs back and forth so she's making cycling motions. This also helps relieve stomach pain associated with gas or colic.

6. Six-month-old babies start to have good control over their arms and grasping motions. Lay a six-month-old baby on her back under a "baby gym" or homemade mobile and help her reach out and grab the hanging objects above her.

7. Take baby for a swim with you. When she gets in the pool she'll splash and kick, and be very active.

TIME FOR MOM

AND

TIME FOR DAD

In this chapter, you'll learn:

✻ How Moms and Dads stay sane ✻ The Golden Rule of Parental Tiredness
✻ How to take charge ✻ How to remember romance

HOW MOMS AND DADS STAY SANE

If you haven't guessed already, being a dad is hard work. It takes up all of your energy, most of your time, and lots of your money. Some dads look up when their kids leave home and wonder where the last 18 years of their lives went. Not only is this not healthy, it's not good parenting.

When you or Mom or both of you leave without baby, there's going to be a fuss, and sometimes it will be more along the lines of a scream. It's hard, but don't let this keep you from some good-quality alone time with yourself or with your partner. Remember, it's better this way for you and the child too. My advice is to try to get the same babysitter each time so that baby doesn't see a new terrifying face every time you and Mom want to catch a movie. Also, get her or him to come over 20 minutes early to play with the little one while you're getting ready to leave. Better yet, put the young one to bed, hand the sitter a movie, and go enjoy yourself while you can. In two or three hours, all that sleep deprivation will catch up with you anyway

If you don't take breaks, get babysitters, and find time for yourself and some romantic dinners with your partner, things will not go according to plan. You'll get way too stressed, angry, tired, and downright bored. Without romance, you and your partner will start to drift apart. This isn't good for anyone—least of all for baby.

When you do make time for yourself and your partner, you'll find time to relax and do grown-up things so that when you're doing kid things you won't lose enthusiasm. Plus, you're setting an important example for your little one on how to make and nurture relationships. The less stressed-out the two of you are, the less stressed-out baby will be. Your sanity is worth preserving.

THE GOLDEN RULE OF PARENTAL TIREDNESS

Here's a rule you need to digest and get into your head pretty quickly: No matter how tired or wiped-out you feel, you never feel as tired and wiped out as your wife. If you need to whine and whinge, call a buddy. That's not to say your wife won't realize that you've been working hard (assuming you have). You just need to reciprocate and recognize her hard work too.

To ensure both of you stay sane, let your wife take time for herself by offering to take care of the baby while she goes out or simply sitting with the baby while she takes a nap. Maybe you can work out a trade—if she watches the baby one night, you'll watch baby the next.

MOM'S GOING OUT!

Scary as being alone with the baby might sound for the beginner dad, this is actually a great opportunity for us dads. Mom gets to go away and decompress by enjoying something totally different (less stressed-out wives equal happier husbands and better relationships all round), baby gets some valuable Dad time (bonding now equals loyalty later on), and you get to show off your prowess as a father (proving once and for all that men can stand on equal footing with women when it comes to caregiving).

There's only one thing you need to worry about and that's the fact that you do not have breasts, or at least the milk-producing kind—a minor cause for alarm if baby is breastfeeding. Then again, if baby has never taken a bottle, there's always a first time for everything. Mom can just pump some breast milk before she leaves and put it in the freezer for you to heat up when baby gets hungry. If all of this sounds frightening, get over it and get used to it. A breast pump might sound like a sex toy, but in fact this wonderful invention can be the means of great liberation for breastfeeding mothers who crave the odd hour of freedom.

Of course, courageous and brave though we may be, it's not a bad idea to make sure you do know where Mom is and that she's not too far away so you can take baby to her or she can come home, if worst comes to worst. This doesn't mean we can't handle the baby alone, it just means nature did not build us the same way. Of course, if baby is bottle-feeding then Mom can be gone for as long as she wants, but don't remind her of this. Being capable does not mean you have to torture yourself.

HOW TO TAKE CHARGE

Taking charge is all about being prepared. Don't think that you can just calmly pick up baby when it's time for Mom to walk out the door and confidently wave goodbye. That will be possible, but you'll first have to do some things to get to that calm and confident place.

First check that you have all the basics such as diapers, food, and toys. Then clear your schedule. There is nothing more frustrating that trying to get something done—a meeting, a phone call, drinks with friends—when you're the only one in the house with baby. For one, babies know what you're trying to do. I don't know how, but instinctively they know that you're not paying attention to them. Then they cry. Try this once and you'll have learnt the lesson for life. So to make matters easy and calm, just don't plan anything except spending time with baby. You'll both be better off for it.

Then, before Mom walks out the door or before she has her first glass of wine, whichever comes first, have her feed baby if she's breastfeeding. That should stave off baby's hunger pains for at least two hours. Also have her brief you. When did baby last eat? Does he have a fresh diaper? Is there breast milk in the freezer or is there formula in the cupboard? How has baby's temperament been all day? Grumpy? Fussy? Crying? Great.

Once you feel like you have enough information, go ahead and pick the child up or start playing with him a good half hour before Mom leaves. Distraction is your best tool here. Get baby playing with something or, even better, sleeping, and then tell him you'll be right back. Go kiss Mom goodbye then let her out the back door. No need for baby to say goodbye. You have everything under control.

PREPARATION FOR WHEN MOM IS OUT

☑ Make sure there are enough diapers in the house so you don't have to head out to the grocery store with a soggy, stinky, and probably tearful baby in tow.

☑ Make sure you have two bottles of breast milk or pre-mixed formula in bottles in the fridge and ready to warm up.

☑ Make sure you know how to warm up a bottle. See page 67 if you need to brush up on these skills.

☑ Make sure there is food in the house for you to eat.

☑ Having a pacifier around is important unless baby likes to suck on your washed pinkie finger. Either one can stand in as a stunt double for Mom's breast or a bottle nipple in an emergency.

☑ Make sure Mom has her cell phone turned on or you know where to get in touch.

SPENDING TIME ALONE WITH BABY

When you're alone with baby, perhaps the one thing you have to remind yourself of often is to slow down and take your time. A baby will get stressed out and upset if you're running around trying to do a hundred things with one hand while the other is holding her. Just commit to the task at hand and abandon any thoughts of working in the yard, watching that action movie, or washing the car. You'll only be disappointed. Besides, this is your chance to bond with your child, not your stuff.

TEN ACTIVITIES FOR DADS AND BABIES

1. Walk around the house while pointing to and naming everything you see.
2. Go for a walk down the street. Don't forget to take baby with you.
3. Sit on the couch and help baby stand up.
4. Go for a drive.
5. Take a nap. But only if baby is taking one too.
6. Stare at baby and smile.
7. Listen to soft music.
8. Make funny noises with your mouth.
9. Sing to baby.
10. Practice the baby exercises your learned in the previous chapter.

TIME FOR YOURSELF

Taking time for yourself can be for various reasons. You might want to catch up with friends at a bar, or go watch a movie, or simply relax and take a drive. It may also be that if you don't pay attention to yourself, your health will start to fail. High stress, little or no sleep, and no exercise will weaken your immune system and invite sickness, not to mention zap creative energy and slow you down at work. And if you feel bad, chances are you're not looking your best either. Bags under the eyes, two-day stubble, and wrinkled clothes are just a few signs that you need to put down the baby and step away from the changing table.

TEN SIGNS YOU NEED HELP

1 You fall asleep under the baby gym while your little one is playing.

2 You show up at work with spit-up stains on your shirt and don't care.

3 Everyone you see asks if there's been a death in the family.

4 Dinner has become your infant's leftover rice cereal.

5 You fall asleep in the drive-through at the fast food restaurant.

6 You freshen yourself up with a diaper wipe.

7 Cold coffee becomes "not that bad."

8 Plants wilt when you breathe on them.

9 You forget your baby's name when the grocery store clerk asks about it.

10 You drive to the doctor's office for the three-month check-up and forget to put the baby in the car.

TIME FOR ROMANCE

With a new baby waking up at all hours of the night and the stresses of work in full swing, lots of things start to fall by the wayside, including house cleaning, yard work, reading the paper, and so many others. During the first years of having a baby, it's also easy to slack off the romantic aspect of the relationship you have with your partner. What's worse is that while the dirty dishes and clothes will visibly stack up, there aren't many overt warning signs that your relationship is going sour. You can expect that your sex life won't be the same for a few months after the birth, if you can find the energy even then. Plus, it'll be no surprise that both of you would rather sleep when the baby is asleep instead of staying up to watch a movie or talk. The danger is that these things continue to happen.

That's why it's important to carve out some time for you and the missus. How, you ask? Initiative, communication, and money.

Take the initiative by bringing home flowers, giving the occasional back rub, and insisting on five minutes to talk and snuggle at the end of each day. Communicate your concern, disappointment, and happiness, and encourage your partner to do the same. Use your money to hire babysitters, house cleaners, and anyone else who can make things a little smoother and free up some time for you and your partner, even if it's just once every two weeks.

Of course, getting a sitter and instigating a date night once a week is what you really want to do. And if you're having trouble fitting it into your schedule then change your schedule. After all, this is the relationship you started with, and when the kids leave home to explore their own lives it'll be the relationship you have in the end. That's the idea anyway. To make it a reality, the relationship is going to need some attention, cultivation, and love.

SOME THINGS YOU CAN DO FOR LOVE

☑ After you put baby down at night, sit with your partner, even if it's just for five minutes, and talk about your day.

☑ Get your parents (or hers) to come round and watch the baby while the two of you have fun and your parents get to practice their grand-parenting skills.

☑ Hire a movie your know your partner wants to watch so that you both feel like you're at least doing something fun on Saturday night after baby has finally got to sleep. Don't forget the ice-cream.

☑ Rub her shoulders, even if it's just for five minutes.

☑ Dress your baby up in a funny costume and have a good laugh together at your child's expense.

☑ Put baby in a stroller and go for walks together.

☑ Take naps together.

☑ Drive through the country together while baby is asleep in the car.

☑ Make dinner together, even if it's cheese toast and canned soup.

☑ Get a babysitter or swap sitting time with other friends who have children. Then go out and make a pact to talk about anything other than your darling baby.

☑ Take a bath with the whole family.

☑ Take Mom and baby on a surprise romantic picnic—even if it's just in the backyard.

ROUND TWO, ANYONE?

With a little creativity, patience, and a big sense of humor, getting through your child's first years won't hurt as bad as you might think. Sure, you'll lose sleep and get out of shape, and the nights out with your buddies won't happen as often. But who really cares? If that's all you have to trade to get that one look of sweet, innocent, unconditional love from your own baby, sign me up.

Many are the fathers who claim to learn something from their young ones. It usually has to do with getting back in touch with that simple and joyful attitude of childhood. "Look at the way he just smiles at everything all the time," you might hear yourself say. Or you might notice that babies can scream as if the world is ending in one moment and the next they can be happily investigating your key ring. It's a great lesson in letting go of what troubles you.

Besides, babyhood will be over in no time. Then you and your wife will be dealing with toddlerhood, which is a whole other ball game. It's only natural, of course. Just don't instal a new pond in your backyard for the next ten years or so.

The bottom line is this: Enjoy your child's infancy. When people say, with a hint of wistfulness, that it goes by so fast, take heed. In the years to come you'll look back fondly, even longingly, for those times when your baby first said "Dada" or got his first teeth. Believe it or not, you'll even miss those late, late nights when you stood in the dark in the wee hours holding your crying baby and helping him manage his new and sometimes scary world. It may even be enough for you and your wife to have that conversation you thought you'd never have: Shouldn't we have another? Fatherhood does something to a man.

INDEX

A

air travel 60–1
allergic reactions 87, 89, 93
anemia 55
antibiotics 89
antibodies 65

B

baby carrier 49
babysitter 128
baths 11, 78–9
bleeding 101
bonding 11, 43, 117
bottle-feeding 54, 55, 65–9
botulism 55
Bradley Method 21, 22–3
breast pump 130
breastfeeding 47, 54, 65, 69, 87,
    89, 92, 130
breathing 35–6
burns 102–3
burping 46, 74, 87, 88

C

Caesarean 31
car seat 25, 56–7
car travel 42, 56–60
cervix 32, 35
changing table 50, 76, 105
chapped lips 87
choking 51, 54–5
circumcision 78
clothing 82–3
colds 92, 93

colic 112
confidence, building child's 10, 43
constipation 91
contractions 28, 32–4
convulsions 87
cot 25, 50
coughing 92
couvade syndrome 17
"crutches" 73
crying 64, 70, 108–13
cuts and grazes 100–1

D

dehydration 87–8, 90, 93
delivery 31, 35–6
diaper changing 75–7, 105
diaper rash 77, 90, 109
diarrhea 89–90
dilating 32, 35
dressing a baby 82–3

E

earache 92
electric sockets 50, 51
electrolytes 88, 90, 93
episiotomy 37
equipment, key 25
exercising baby 124–5

F

family, visits by 23, 28, 34
feeding 65–9, 70
fevers 93–7
fingernails 104

first aid 100–3
fetal monitor 36
fontanelle, sunken 87
food poisoning 89
food safety 54–5
formula 64–9
friends, visits by 22, 28, 34

G

gas
  baby suffering from 45, 88, 91, 112
  during pregnancy 15
gate, safety 51
going out 39

H

highchair 51, 55
holding a baby 43–9
home, preparation of 20, 24–5
honey 55
hospital bag 30
hospital births 28, 30
hot water temperature 51
houseplants 51
hygiene 55, 90
hyperventilation 35

I

illness 86–105
immunization 93
injuries 100–5
insurance 23

L

labor 28, 31–8
  active phase 31, 32
  early phase 31, 32
  transitional phase 31, 32–4
  what to say and do 31
Lamaze Method 21, 22
logistics and preparations 20

M

massage
  baby 122–3
  mother 16, 31, 34
morning sickness 15, 16, 17
  expectant fathers 17
mucus in stool 89
music 121
myths about fatherhood 10

N

name, selection 23
nitrates 55
nose, runny 74, 92
nursery 20, 24–5

O

organic food 55

P

paternity leave 20
photographs, taking 30, 37, 38
placenta 31, 37
play 116–21
  group games 120
poisonous substances 50, 51
postnatal depression 39
pregnancy
  fatigue 15
  first trimester 15
  helping your partner 14–16, 23

hormonal changes 15

indigestion 15

mood swings 15

second trimester 15

sex during 18–19

third trimester 15

vomiting 15, 16

weight gain 16

prenatal classes 20, 21–3, 36

R

rocking chair 25, 72

romance, time for 138–9

S

safety precautions 41–61, 73, 104–5

scalding 51

sex during pregnancy 18–19

shaken baby syndrome 10

sleep

getting baby to sleep 72–3

sleeping patterns 70–1

sling 49

slippery rugs 51

smell, heightened sense of 15

stair safety 51

sterilizer 67

sudden infant death syndrome (SIDS) 100, 105

suffocation, danger of 50, 51, 100, 105

sunburn 102–3

T

taking charge 132–4

talcum powder 77

teaching baby 121

teething 90, 93, 98–9, 109

temperature, checking 93–7

thermometers 94–7

time out, taking 128–30, 135

tiredness, parental 129

toys 50

travel, safety precautions 42, 56–61

U

umbilical cord 36, 78

urine

color 69

infrequent 87

uterus 15

V

vaginal canal 32

vaginal tearing 37

video recorder 30

visitors 23, 28, 34

vomiting

by baby 74, 87–8

during pregnancy 15, 16

W

water, bottled 68

weight gain

baby's 69

parents' 16, 17, 23